CROWOOD EQUESTRIAN GUIDES

Basic Dressage

BARBARA RIPMAN

107

The Crowood Press

First published in 1991 by
The Crowood Press Ltd
Ramsbury, Marlborough
Wiltshire SN8 2HR

This impression 1996

© The Crowood Press 1998

British Library Cataloguing-in-Publication Data

Ripman, Barbara
  Basic dressage.
  1. Dressage
  I. Title
  798.23

  ISBN 1 85223 535 7

Disclaimer:
Throughout this book, the pronouns 'he', 'him' and 'his' have
been used inclusively and are meant to apply to both males and
females.

Acknowledgements:
Photographs by Louis Milburn.
Line-drawings by Hazel Morgan.

Typeset by Footnote Graphics, Warminster, Wiltshire
Printed and bound in Great Britain by J. W. Arrowsmith Limited, Bristol

CONTENTS · 3

Basic Dressage is intended as a follow on to *Basic Training* (also published by The Crowood Press) and is written for those who wish to take on the challenge of this discipline.

Although the task involves great skill and learning, the rider must have a clear understanding of the requirements for performing the job well, and giving a good account of himself. The rewards and satisfaction achieved will totally outweigh the hours of hard work and dedication the job requires.

However, it must be remembered that throughout all the horse's training, the basic requirements must be practised well so that they are never forgotten. This will form the basis of all the more advanced work, and will enable horse and rider to proceed in a clear and uncomplicated way to whatever level they might be capable of.

A horse and rider enjoying dressage.

OBJECTIVES OF LESSONS

The development of the horse for dressage is something that can take many years to perfect and even then this may not be totally achieved. After the horse is established in its basic training and has reached a level where it is accepting and submitting to the wishes of the rider (and able to work in a rounded outline relevant to the young or novice horse) we can then proceed further.

The trainer must try to improve his horse in a progressive way, choosing weak or undeveloped points to work on and to improve in a lesson. It would not be possible to cover all these points at one time so the lessons must be planned and divided in order that time can be spent on individual weaknesses.

REQUIREMENTS OF THE DRESSAGE HORSE

Some of the requirements of the young or novice horse at this level must include the following and work must be done in the lessons to try to produce these results:

1. To move freely forward in a natural manner, showing good impulsion at all paces.
2. To be under control, accepting the contact of the hand with light submission, producing a rounded outline relevant to the standard of training.
3. To be responsive and attentive to the rider's aids without the use of great strength or force.
4. To show balanced and supple movement in all his work.
5. To show rhythm and regularity of steps at all paces, producing lengthening and shortening with fluency and ease.

All these requirements are relevant to each other and it is not possible to isolate one point and work totally on that, as it would neglect other equally important points and not develop a complete horse capable of giving all requirements to the best of his ability.

It is, therefore, very important that the trainer be aware of the necessary requirements of the dressage horse and plan a training programme to cover them all, but in a flexible manner.

A novice horse well engaged with the rider in a light seat.

It is never possible to foresee how long a horse will take to learn each part of a lesson as they are all individuals and what one finds easy another will find difficult. It follows that the training plan must be flexible so that any points needing extra time or repeated reference can be allowed for in order that they become well established in the horse's mind.

PROGRAMME OF A WORK SESSION

A lesson or training session might take the following format.

The warm-up period is obviously necessary to stretch and relax muscles to enable the horse to work in a supple and free manner. Provided the horse is not over-fresh, this is best started with a period of walk. The horse should be urged forward in energetic strides and he should be kept on a long rein to encourage the head and neck forward and down. The canter is a very good pace to supple and warm up the horse as it demands more from him than the trot and involves greater muscle activity throughout the horse. If possible this should be carried out again in the long outline and, to prove beneficial, the rider can adopt a light forward seat to encourage the raising and rounding of the horse's back. When returning to trot from this period of canter, it is usually found that the horse has relaxed and stretched through his back and is then more established, in a round position with a lower head carriage.

This warm-up session can be followed with a period of walk to allow the horse a breather before work continues.

The next period of the lesson must be the work period and must contain the exercises the rider feels are necessary to improve the horse's manner of going. For this he can be taken on to a shorter rein contact but not necessarily a stronger one and then encouraged to work to this contact. The amount of shortening depends on the stage that the horse's training has reached: the novice adopting an outline suitable to carry out controlled work at active working paces; the elementary horse and upwards coming more into a collected outline where he must adopt a shorter shape necessitating shorter and more elevated steps.

Whichever stage of training the horse is at, it is possible to practise a little at working and also at collected paces, alternating between the two, depending on the shapes and movements being ridden. The novice horse attempting collection will obviously be a long way from true collection.

This part of the lesson will also include work on circles, turns and straights to both left and right to ensure that both 'sides' of the horse become as equal as possible. Quite often a stiffness is found to one direction more than the other and work must be included to 'soften' the stiff side to produce equality. Horse and rider must work through this period with enthusiasm and, if a stage is reached where the horse has worked well and perhaps beyond the trainer's expectations, then he must get his reward. The rider could follow with less demands and, perhaps, take the horse off for a ride in the fields to let him relax and enjoy himself after his special efforts. Always be flexible in this way because to make any lesson over-demanding will never produce a horse that is happy in his work.

This concentrated work period will take up the largest part of the lesson and must include as much variety as possible, with frequent changes of tempo and direction. Do not be tempted to push a novice into a position that proves too difficult for him to cope with as this will only produce resistances and teach the horse to fight the rider's wishes. Try to make his tasks easy ones within his capabilities.

Spend the final stage of the lesson relaxing the horse and cooling him off so that he returns to the stable happy in both body and mind.

The event horse showing a rounded outline and good trot.

PURE DRESSAGE

Some riders train their horses for dressage purely for personal achievement and the artistic pleasure of trying to perfect movements. These days the majority of riders prefer to train with competition in mind. However, knowing when the horse is ready for his first competition is not an easy task as each will respond differently and be quite unpredictable. Once the rider feels he has the horse under control at all three paces and finds the riding of simple movements fairly easy, then it is a good idea to take the horse to any small local shows to see how he will react and to try to get him to concentrate on his work as reliably as when at home. In addition, it does not hurt a horse to compete in small jumping events as this will also assist him in his physical development as well as keep his mind busy.

DRESSAGE FOR THE EVENT HORSE

These days eventing has become increasingly popular and being able to carry out a good dressage test has become a necessity to achieve any degree of success. The event horse

The event horse showing a more hollow outline and poorer strides.

has to be produced in very good condition, being fit enough to gallop across country and jump a good course of fences but, at the same time, being able to work in a relaxed enough manner for the dressage. This can cause problems for the trainer, especially with the thoroughbred type of horse which is bred to gallop and, once in a very fit condition, it can then be increasingly difficult for him to perform his dressage. However, provided the rider allows the horse to put a great deal of energy and effort into his work on the flat, this can be overcome. Should he be constantly restricted and pulled at, he will get increasingly frustrated at not being allowed to use his energy. To overcome this, he must be asked, or allowed, to put his energy into his flat work so that, after being schooled for his dressage he feels as much satisfaction over the effort used as if he had been schooled over a course of jumps. This then produces a horse with a contented and satisfied mind for dressage.

During the following chapters, the progressive training of the horse will be covered in detail to help the rider produce a horse capable of performing in a correct and athletic manner, from novice through to medium level. This will include the movements requiring both forwards and sideways steps and the further development of collection and balance in the horse.

PROPORTIONS AND DIMENSIONS OF ARENAS

Riding in a correctly proportioned arena can both assist the trainer in his schooling and accustom him to the size and confines of it until riding within its size, while performing movements and turns, becomes second nature.

All dressage arenas are of set dimensions, the smaller one being 20m×40m and the larger 20m×60m. The 20m circle fits into the 20×20m square and this is thought to be an ideal size for schooling both the novice and advanced horse.

When schooling is carried out in a field, it takes a very experienced rider to recognize and ride correct dimensions, so an arena size must be marked out reasonably correctly. The use of jump poles laid on the ground with cones as markers can indicate the perimeter of the arena and they are easily moved. For the riding of movements it is necessary to put the markers in the correct places and letter sequences.

SHAPES AND MOVEMENTS RIDDEN WITHIN THE ARENA

Accuracy of shapes and movements within the arena is very important and is only achieved by practice and self-discipline. As both rider and horse develop this technique and balance improves, it is then possible to ride smaller shapes and turns. The variety and variation of shapes that can be used by the expert rider are numerous and can prove to be both stimulating and enjoyable, keeping horse and rider interested and occupied in their work.

SOME BASIC SCHOOL MOVEMENTS EXPLAINED

Going Large   Riding the perimeter of the arena which consists of straight lines and corners. Through the corners the horse should be bent to the direction of the curve. A novice will be kept to a shallow curve and only taken deeper into the corners as schooling advances.

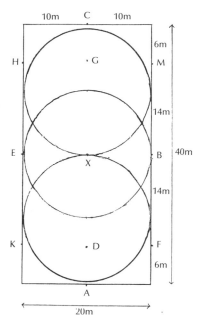

The 20m × 40m arena. Three 20m circles will fit into this arena, and with young or novice horses the corners are ridden as a quarter of the 20m circle.

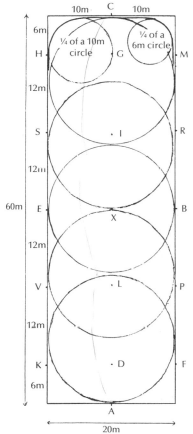

The 20m × 60m arena. Five 20m circles will fit into this arena. The more advanced the horse is, the deeper the corners are ridden – the diagram shows a quarter of a 10m circle and a quarter of a 6m circle.

Some basic school movements.

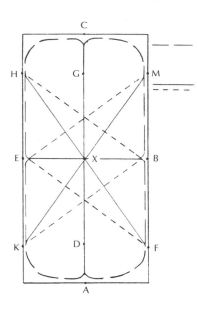

Changes of rein on diagonal lines.

Three-loop and four-loop serpentines.

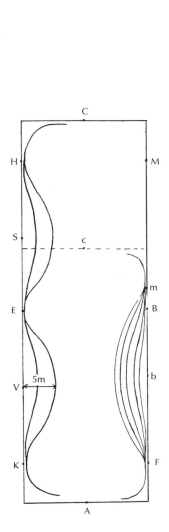

Single or double loops are used in the 40m and 60m arenas. These vary from 1m to 5m in depth.

20m Circle Must be of this size and consist of one continuous curving line with the horse curved to the perimeter line of that circle.

Half 20m Circle Half of the 20m circle; these can be linked together to form figures of eight and serpentines, the number depending on the length of the arena. When the direction of the half-circle is changed, then so must the bend of the horse to relate to the curve of the new half-circle. To perform this well the horse must be in the upright throughout its execution.

Loops The simplest of these is the single loop, performed on the long side of the arena. This starts in the corner coming out of the short side. The horse is led from the track into the arena, the maximum depth being reached by the half-marker and then he is returned to the track by the corner at the other end of the long side. When ridden in the walk or trot, the bend must be changed as direction is changed. When ridden in the canter, the bend is maintained to that of the leading leg and the bend is not changed unless the leading leg is changed.

At first, loops should be kept to approximately 1m deep and increased as balance improves. In the 20 × 60m arena this exercise can consist of two loops of equal depth, the first finishing by the half-marker and the second at the end of the long side. This exercise can assist the horse's upright posture and straighten him.

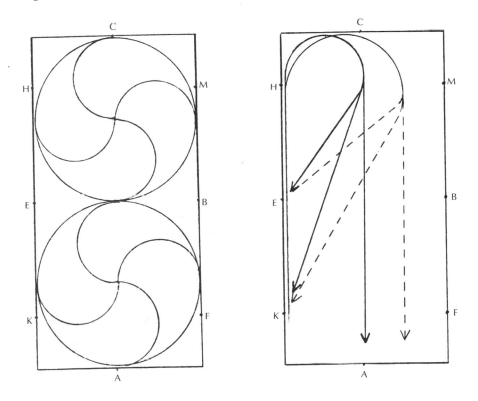

Change of Rein   Can be carried out in numerous ways. Diagonal lines of varying angles and lengths, turns to left and right across the arena, half-circles left and right through large circles or across the arena, turns on the forehand and the haunches (half-pirouettes); in fact anywhere where the horse can be taken to the opposite direction and the bend through the horse changed.

The importance of all school work is the precision and correctness of its execution. Nothing is achieved by the rider who trots aimlessly around the arena with no direction or purpose.

Left: changing rein through the large half-circles and 10m half-circles. Combinations of these can create serpentines through the length of either the 40m or 60m arenas.

Right: changing rein through the half 10m or 15m circle and returning to the track on the long or short diagonals or on the centre line.

Certain requirements are essential in the riding of turns, circles and movements, which will enhance quality and execution.

ACCURACY

This can make or destroy other qualities involving direction of movement. It is a necessity. Quality and execution is totally dependent on the rider, whether the movements be simple, as in a 20m circle, or more intricate, as those involving the more advanced horse. This exactness is even more necessary when test riding. Marks can be thrown away by incorrect shapes and the inaccuracy of the lines ridden. The discipline of accurate riding must be practised in a regular manner at home. It would be wrong to expect correct responses if they are only asked for on special occasions. The value of accurate, well-ridden shapes can be immense, giving quality to what might be rather ordinary work.

BALANCE

The balanced horse will be able to perform all his movements in a manner that will make them look easy and harmonious. The regular execution of movements will also improve the horse's carriage, enabling him to take more weight on his quarters rather than his forehand, so helping him develop self-carriage. The most dramatic effect is seen when the horse is able to carry himself with more upright posture, so correcting any tendency to lean to left or right through turns and circles. Total balance is only achieved when coupled with the balanced rider, thus enabling them to perform in complete harmony through all turns and movements.

RHYTHM AND TEMPO

This must be maintained in a regular manner throughout all school work. Its practice is obviously easier on large shapes than on smaller, more intricate ones and it is only the rider's awareness of rhythm during his work that can develop the flow of uninterrupted energy necessary for their correct execution.

Horse and rider cantering in an upright posture.

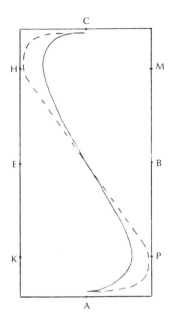

The solid line indicates a poor change of rein; the dotted line is correct.

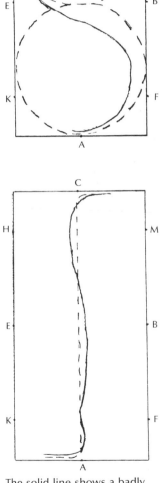

The solid line shows a bad change of circle; the dotted line is correct.

FIGURE RIDING

For figure riding to have the desired qualities, it is not sufficient to ride merely from one marker to another, but instead a mental picture must be made of the shape of the movement so that it flows with one line linking smoothly with the next. Some riders find this feeling for shape hard to imagine or achieve. They can sometimes be helped by taking a pen and paper and drawing the required shape to see how it fits within the arena size. These drawn pictures must then be kept in the mind throughout the riding sessions, with the rider knowing exactly the make-up of each shape and its requirements of curves and straights. When these techniques are then used for test riding, the appearance is not one of the rider breaking up the test into individual bits but rather of a feeling of rhythmical movement with one shape connecting to the next. The numerous shapes and turns that can be ridden within the arena must be used to give interest and variety to schooling sessions. It must be understood and realized how each shape and direction can be used to improve or better the horse's manner of going and so further his training.

The solid line shows a badly ridden centre line; the dotted line is correct.

STRONGER RIDING POSITION

As training progresses, the rider's posture must have an increased influence over the horse, helping to produce more controlled energy, hence affecting the carriage of the horse and the balance through his work.

This rider is adopting a heavy, slumped position, totally unsuitable for stimulating the horse.

During this period the horse must be ridden increasingly in the sitting trot. By this action of sitting, the rider should be able to make himself more effective on the horse and so produce more engagement and energy. When first introduced, the rider must not sit in too strong or too heavy a manner as this can cause undue strain on the horse's back and will tend to spoil the trot rather than improve it. From a balanced position in the rising trot, the rider must start to sit but only for short periods in the initial stages. What is important is the manner and the position adopted by the rider. He must be capable of keeping a tall, upright position with a lightly braced back, so helping the horse at this stage by not sitting too deeply or too powerfully in the saddle, which would only tire his back. This tall, light position is very important with the more thoroughbred type of horse as these have a tendency to become worried and tense by the effect of a strong, very powerful drive from the rider. There are, however, many horses that will need this more powerful type of riding and the rider must be capable of riding in either position to deal with the individual horse.

ADAPTING THE POSITION TO SUIT THE JOB

To attain this more powerful position, the rider should adopt a body posture that is still straight and tall but, by bracing the position a little behind the vertical and pushing the pelvis deeper and slightly towards the front of the saddle, he is able to have a much stronger influence in the production of forward energy. However, there is a point where, if the rider takes the

(a)   (b)

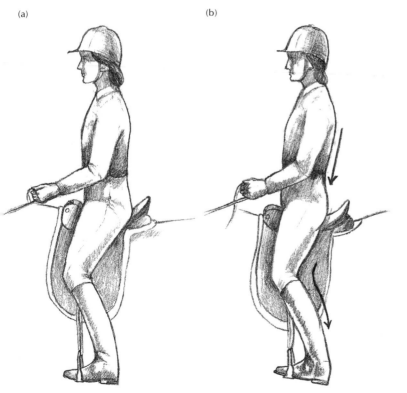

Body position: (a) the rider is in a tall, upright position; (b) the rider is in a braced position.

shoulders too far behind the vertical and tends to over-relax the muscles of the back into a slightly curved, banana-shaped posture, he loses the ability to carry and balance his body. The result is that he then rides behind the movement and so becomes a passenger that is hanging back from the forward movement. The resistance caused by this position can dissuade the horse from active forward work and the rider is then seen to lean even further back, thinking this will improve the driving aids. In fact, the more this is done, the more inactive it makes the horse. To prevent this from happening it is always necessary to adopt a tall, supple position with the shoulders only *slightly* behind the vertical and only taken further back if a more bracing action is required for downward transitions or, with a more powerful horse, in the half-halt action.

This rider is adopting a poor riding posture with a rounded body and drawn up legs.

The same rider in a taller body posture and a better leg position.

When correctly executed the sitting trot will improve the horse's carriage and activity; it should not cause him in any way to hollow his back and raise his head and neck. Should this happen at any time, then the rising trot must be resumed to give the horse's back the rest it needs. The sitting trot should then be reintroduced only for short periods until he is stronger and more developed.

HAND AND LEG POSITIONS

From the sitting posture the rider is also able to increase the efficiency and effectiveness of his legs which can be applied with every stride rather than every other stride, as in the rising trot. The leg aids must not only be capable of producing energy, but by their correct positioning and action, they can also direct and help to control it. For maximum efficiency they must always be placed correctly in position, and at this stage it should be possible for the rider to adopt a slightly longer stirrup in order to keep his legs long on the horse's sides and

This rider has collapsed in the waist to the right and is out of balance with the horse.

(a)　　　　　　　　　　　(b)

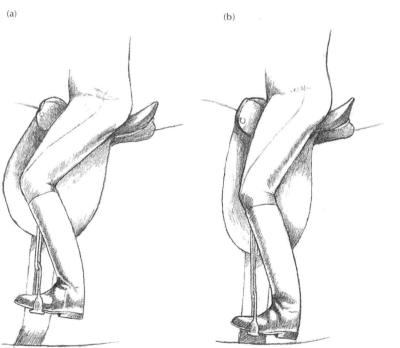

Leg position: (a) The general-purpose leg position in a general-purpose saddle; (b) a longer leg position in a dressage saddle.

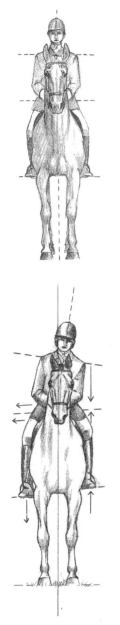

If a rider tilts to one side by dropping his shoulders towards his hip, he will affect the balance and movement of the horse.

so use them to the full. They must keep a close contact through as much of their length as possible and from this position only a minimum amount of movement is necessary to create maximum results. The rider should always avoid excessive movement of his legs as this can look unsightly and will only deaden the horse's responses. Far better to support a lighter leg aid with the schooling whip or a pair of spurs. Artificial aids must never replace the natural aids but they can prove very helpful in supporting them.

Good body posture, helped by efficient leg aids, will assist the collection of the horse. This necessitates a bracing of the back and a firm leg action. The body posture will again play an important role. When lengthening is required, the back muscles will assist the movement but this time the seat is pressed down and forward into the saddle to stimulate the forward energy, helped by firm leg aids. In this driving position the rider must take care not to be left behind the horse as he steps into the more energetic strides. The body must not lie back at this moment as then the balance will be lost throughout the whole lengthening.

Balance is also very important from left to right and the rider must take care not to lean or collapse in the waist in any one direction as this can cause a counter-action from the horse which will prevent him from working in an upright and balanced position. The full effect of any lean or lack of balance will be seen when the horse is put into movements such as counter canter when he will be prevented from executing the movements correctly.

As the horse is increasingly worked in collection, his head and neck carriage will become higher. With this action the rider's hands must be raised gradually so as to maintain the straight line from the horse's mouth along the rein, through the forearm to the elbow. The rider's arm and hand position must try to achieve the ideal but it will not be possible through all the riding sessions. There will be times when it will be necessary to lower them back to the more novice position, just above the wither, until a lesson is learned or corrected. Once this is achieved, the higher hand position can be resumed. It must be remembered that any raising of the hands must not affect the contact down the rein by an increase or decrease of its feel. Should the rider require more contact in the hand, it must be produced by the action of the legs, seat and back, so sending the horse into the contact of the bit.

A good posture is not only essential for correct riding but is a delight to see, and its effect on a horse will produce a balanced ride, showing athletic and gymnastic qualities without the use of tough or rough actions.

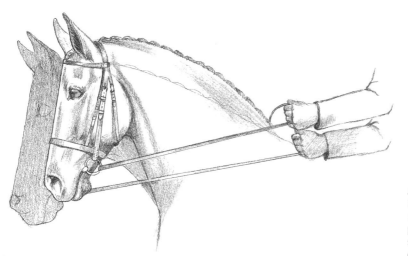

As the horse develops a high head and neck carriage, the rider can raise his hand position to maintain the straight line from bit to elbow.

As the horse's head and neck are carried higher so the rider's hands can be also.

RIDING CIRCLES AND SERPENTINES

Working the horse in a more engaged and active manner through the use of seat and back aids, should begin to produce the start of collection. This must only be practised or, in fact, expected, for short periods as it is not until the horse reaches (probably) medium level that he is capable of sustaining this quality of work for any length of time. While the horse is engaged in any concentrated work, it must be punctuated by periods of walk where he must be allowed to stretch his outline to the fullest extent, relaxing muscles that are unaccustomed to the strains and demands being asked.

During this exacting work the rider must not concentrate too much on one thing but plan programmes that improve both the horse's and his own skills.

SIZE OF CIRCLES

Once the horse is capable of maintaining his balance on the large and simple shapes of circles, serpentines and so on, he must start to lessen the size of these shapes and learn to keep the same balance and suppleness during this more concentrated work. This is a gradual process, reducing circles from

Right to left: horse and rider upright and in balance to the 10m circle.

20m to 15m and subsequently to 12m and 10m. The smallest circle ('volte') that the horse is expected to perform is of 6m but this is in the later, more advanced stages of his training. With the novice, the half 10m circle, progressing to the full 10m circle is all that is necessary and through its execution he will be able to perform a variety of turns and shapes relevant to future work. The riding of circles, however large or small, must become a practised art as, if performed correctly, they improve and assist the horse's education. However, when faults creep in or are allowed to persist, the objective of circle work is lost.

HORSE'S POSITION ON CIRCLES

To be correct on a circle, the horse must travel around its perimeter with his body bent, from his head through to his tail, to match exactly the curve of the circle. He must, at the same time, be capable of remaining in the upright without leaning to left or right. Only when he is in this upright position is he both balanced and bent correctly for the circle. The rider must be careful that he is not deceived by the horse in this work by allowing small faults to creep in; one such fault being the horse that evades the true bend to the circle by pushing his quarters away to the outside. The rider can help to prevent this

This rider is slipping to the outside with the inside leg drawn up and back.

by keeping his outside leg in a backward, passive position. This should prove sufficient to stop the fault occurring, but should it be a more established habit, then the rider must correct it by moving the shoulders out in front of the quarters. This correction can be carried out by maintaining and using a firm inside leg on the girth, helped by the outside rein moving slightly away from the neck to take the shoulders away in that same direction. The inside rein can be closed to the neck to support the action but must not cross over the neck to the far side. At the same time it will continue to ask for bend to the direction of the circle. These combined actions of legs and hands will then produce a balanced and upright horse bending around the circle.

POSITION FOR RIDING CIRCLES

The discipline of the rider during circle work is very important and he must assist the horse both with his position and his actions. As when riding on the straight, he must sit in an equally balanced way astride the horse, not leaning in or out. His aids must be firm or passive depending on the requirements of the horse but he must be fully aware of his actions.

Top: the horse's bend should match the circle, however, sometimes the horse will evade the bend by moving his quarters out.

Bottom: if the horse falls into a circle through his inside shoulder, he will also have to adopt a bend to the outside.

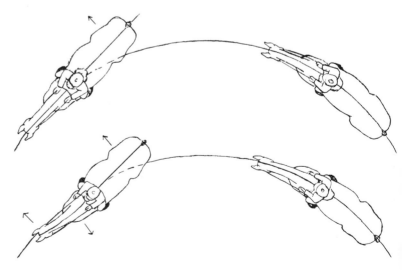

On a circle it is not uncommon, especially at the slightly faster paces of trot and canter, for the rider to be pushed away from the circle by the centrifugal forces prevalent in this form of exercise. This will affect both horse and rider and the rider might feel he is slipping to the outside, sometimes to the extent that he feels the saddle slip to the outside. This tendency will affect the rider's position by making him draw his inside leg upwards, so accentuating his lean to the outside. To prevent this and keep in balance, he must keep a long stretched feel to his inside leg and must try to push the foot down towards the ground. Should this habit persist, then it can help the rider if he occasionally quits the inside stirrup and allows his leg to hang in as long a position as possible.

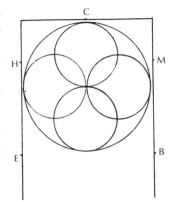

Riding 10m circles within the 20m circle.

The introduction and the riding of the 10m half and full circles will give the rider a greater range of work to conduct with the horse. It can involve riding from the large 20m circle on to the 10m circle, or the half 10m circle into the centre of the 20m circle and then returning to its perimeter on the other 10m half-circle. This half-circle left and right is a good way of testing the horse's balance through the change of rein. Half 10m circles can be made to the centre line and then the horse put on the diagonal line back to the track which will again change the rein. Serpentines can be ridden, but now involving 10m and 12m half-circles instead of 20m, so practising more frequent changes of direction which will prove more testing for the horse.

When being ridden from one half-circle to another, the horse must stay in the upright during the change of direction; its performance being spoilt if he is allowed to fall from one direction into the other.

When riding any circle, the actions of the rider must be to push the horse from the inside leg into the outside hand, so helping to create the correct bend through the body to the inside. Before changing to a new direction, the horse must momentarily be taken into the straight and the upright position to help avoid any lean or fall of his body-weight. This moment of straight allows him a second or two to balance himself before the new bend is taken. By riding circles to both directions the rider will make the horse equal. However, these concentrated exercises must not be overpractised as they can tire and strain the horse. A variety of work must, therefore, be included in the overall lesson.

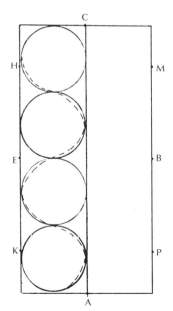

Serpentines are formed if 10m circles from the long side of the arena are looped together.

Throughout the complete training of the horse the aids do not change; they are always transmitted through the feel of hands, legs, seat and voice, assisted by the artificial aids of whip and spurs. However, the responses the horse makes to the rider's aids must improve to produce greater energy and easier control throughout his programme of work.

The strength used when applying the aids will depend on two main factors. The first is the sensitivity of the horse – some responding easily to very light aids and others requiring much greater stength to create both activity and control. The second

This horse is more engaged in an improved outline.

is the individual strength and physique of each rider and the application of the aids.

As training advances the application of the aids must be more economical and correct, always applied initially in the same position and with the same strength; only then can they produce the same result on each occasion.

With the more schooled horse, the aids will become less obtrusive, with the rider making more use of his back, seat and weight to influence both energy and its direction. This will result in the horse becoming increasingly responsive to any shift in weight to left or right and, when coupled with the appropriate leg aids, can instantly give the desired result.

At this stage the rider must resist any temptation to produce energy by any over-exaggerated movement of his body, as this can destroy freedom and movement rather than enhancing it.

The contact of the hands on the reins must also be refined so that the feels they produce are very controlled. This can only be done by a rider capable of maintaining a good balanced position. It must always be remembered that, should a rider require a stronger feel on the reins, it must be produced by first sending the horse forward from the driving aids to enable him to take the extra feel with the hands.

The majority of riding practised so far will have been forward stimulated, with the restraint taken on the reins only being sufficient to enable the rider to have control over his horse. So, prior to the introduction of the restraining action necessary for the half halt, the rider must ensure that the horse fully understands these forward driving aids and will produce forward energy when asked. To ensure this, he must be made very responsive to the action of the rider's legs which should have a more stimulating effect on him. If this is not forthcoming and the responses given are not energetic or sharp enough, the rider must rectify it immediately.

It might be necessary, with a lazy or sluggish horse, to stimulate him with the assistance of a schooling whip, applying it with sharp taps in rhythm to the strides. Even with the very idle types, this will normally provide the necessary response. At this time the rider should avoid the temptation to apply the legs with a hard kicking or thumping action as it will seldom produce the desired effect. Remember, most novice horses' lack of response is quite often due to the lack of understanding of the leg aids rather than disobedience to them.

With the added stimulation being provided by the schooling whip, the leg aid can be stronger but not excessive as the horse might interpret this action as normal and expect it all the time, which would become very tiring for the rider. Teach him instead to move off a light leg aid and learn to pay attention to its messages.

To assist these driving actions, the rider must also become more effective with the use of his seat and lower back, using the latter to produce more swing to the strides. These actions should keep the horse working in front of the rider's legs and stepping out ahead of him, so preventing any tendency to drop back from the bridle into the rider, giving the impression of the rider toppling forward over the front of the horse.

This type of forward work will encourage the horse into the contact of the bit and produce a good feel in the rider's hands without pulling or backing off their contact.

Once a horse has learned to accept and work to the contact of the hands and is willing to assume a submissive attitude to their action, then he can be taught the half halt.

THE HALF HALT

The half halt can have a number of uses, one of these being to make the horse take an equal feel on both reins. It is quite often found that the horse is stronger to one side of his mouth than the other and it is to this firm side that the half halt is given to try to lighten it to match the other. During its application the rider must ensure that the horse continues with energetic forward movement. Best executed in the trot, short restraining actions can be taken on the hard side of the mouth, each time following with a lighter feel, whilst a firmer feel is taken on the opposite rein. Gradually, through regular use, it can make the feel to both sides of the mouth equal which will subsequently be necessary to make the horse straight.

The most regular use of the half halt is to prepare the horse for the next movement, transition, turn and so on. It will give the horse notice that something is going to happen. When used in this context, the forward drive must be ensured by seat and leg aids, and a short firm restraint should be taken on the reins while the body assists this action by a bracing of the back muscles. In the instant the horse responds to this action, the

To move the horse both forwards and sideways he must be more response to the aids.

rider must yield the hand and ensure the horse continues forward in an active manner from the driving aids. Later, when more collection is wanted, this action can assist the rider in shortening the horse's outline for this work. The action of the half halt must be repeated as frequently as necessary to produce the desired results.

If, during its application, the horse shows any tendency to raise the head or neck into a hollow or resistant outline, he is not ready to receive this aid. The rider must then return to more basic work to establish it in a more thorough manner.

THE FULL HALT

The full halt is first executed in a progressive way; that is to say making the horse come gradually into the halt through lesser paces and shortened strides. He must be kept straight through the transition and encouraged to stand square. At the first attempts, if he comes into the halt with little resistance and stands still calmly, then he must be rewarded as this forms the basis of a good halt.

From this stage he must be encouraged to engage the hind legs more underneath him as he comes into the halt so standing with his weight equally distributed over his four legs 'square'. This is achieved by the rider closing his legs on the horse's sides as the hands take the restraint necessary on the reins, supported by the braced back position with the body. This combination will bring the horse into the halt. He must then be allowed to stand calmly in a 'four square' posture. Should this transition be asked for with the reins too long, then the rider may be left behind the movement with his hands raised too high in an attempt to restrain the forward movement. This action can only result in the horse raising his head and neck and hollowing his back, when he will come to the

The full halt. This rider is in a light seat coming in to the halt and is relying too much on his reins. The result is that the horse comes behind the vertical.

halt with the hind legs left out behind him. Once in the halt the rider must allow the horse to stand, never rushing him to move off again.

In the early stages, it is wrong to pay too much attention to minor defects such as whether the position of the legs is absolutely square, as this can destroy the horse's confidence and he will start to fidget which then causes the rider additional problems.

Performed well, the more advanced horse should be capable of the canter to halt transition with fluency and ease of movement, showing no signs of strong aids which result in abrupt responses.

The full halt. This rider is in a braced position which engages the horse from behind so that he comes to a halt with lowered quarters and a more raised forehand.

The full halt. This rider is hauling backward on a long rein and a forward leg. This causes the horse to hollow his back and raise his head and neck.

The rein back. The rider's braced back assists the contact taken on the reins and both his legs are taken behind the girth.

THE REIN BACK

The rein back can be started quite early on in the education of the horse even if it is only one or two strides taken in a relaxed manner.

The movement is started from a good halt and the horse should step back, moving his legs in diagonals as in the trot. The true diagonals must be picked up and fluently placed backwards, making a clean lift and step. They should not be dragged or shuffled backwards.

The very first attempts must be taken slowly with the horse not being rushed, pulled or kicked, causing tension and the resulting resistant, hollow horse that refuses to move.

When first introduced, it can help to have a little assistance from the ground, making the job simpler. Once in the halt, the rider should maintain a light but fairly short rein contact; if the rein is left long the rider might be tempted to lean back too much when the restraint is applied to it. In the first attempts at this movement, the rider must at least stay in the upright even if it becomes necessary to slightly lighten the seat in the saddle by allowing the body to move forward a little.

From the halt the rider should take his legs lightly backwards along the horse's sides until they are placed well behind the girth where they are not applied for any other aid. They must then be placed lightly on the horse's sides while the hands, via the reins, ask for the steps backwards. If the legs are applied to strongly the horse can become confused, thinking he must step forward but not being allowed to by the hands. He can then refuse to move anywhere, becoming tense and resistant.

In the first attempt, the assistant on the ground can stand to the front of the horse and apply his hand to the front of the chest or shoulder and, with a little pressure or tapping action, urge him to step back, using the voice to assist these actions where necessary. Even if the first step or steps are limited, perhaps only moving one leg a short way, then immediately relax the aids and praise the horse, and then apply the same aids again. If the horse shows any confusion then walk him forward, halt again and then apply the aids once more but using the help of an assistant.

The horse learns the rein back quickly in this manner without tension and resistance, the result being that once learned in this way all the rider must do from the halt is place his legs lightly in the reverse position, ask with the restraining hands for the steps back, and assist these actions with a slight backward brace of the back to produce a smoothly executed movement without the use of force or strength.

Once learned, the rein back can assist in improving the horse's balance, helping to place the hind legs further under him so engaging them for the upward transitions.

In training it is not necessary to hurry forward immediately after the steps back; it can be more beneficial to allow some horses to halt before making the upward transition. This can give them a moment to stand and compose themselves prior to engaging forward. If this moment is not allowed the rein back can become ragged and incomplete, with the horse not having time to complete the strides backward in a calm manner before being asked to move forward again.

The rein back when well executed should be a fluent movement, carried out with the horse in a round, submissive outline, taking regular diagonal steps backwards, from where he is then ready to make the upward transition into any forward pace with balance and ease.

The rein back. Good positive diagonal strides with no resistance in the mouth.

RHYTHM AND TEMPO

The rhythm and tempo through the three basic paces must be developed and improved with the progression of training. The rider must always be aware and have an understanding of these two requirements.

WALK

The Free Walk This is a four-time rhythm where the horse must take unrestricted, long strides. Should the rider over-drive the walk and quicken its step sequence, the rhythm will be lost. The length and sequence of the strides will be disrupted, sometimes even destroying the correct leg sequence.

Free walk.

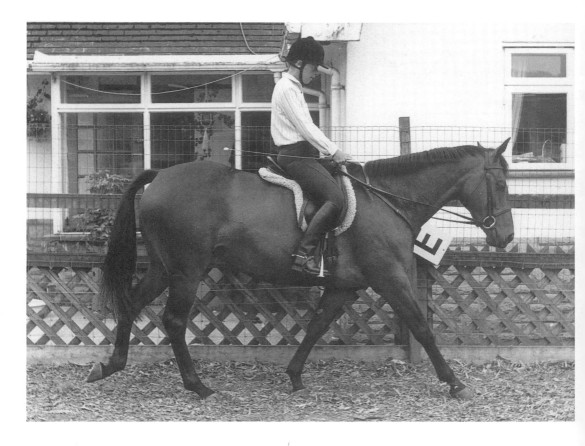

Should an incorrect leg sequence be allowed to develop and become a habit, the horse will appear to 'pace' by moving the lateral legs forward at the same time. This can be a very difficult problem to correct and can totally spoil the walk.

The Collected Walk   The same problem can also be seen in the collected walk where it is often caused by over-collection for too long a period which over-shortens the steps, having the same results. For this reason care must be taken when collecting the walk and it should only be practised for short periods, perhaps just prior to a transition being made. The action of collection not only shortens the outline of the horse but his strides as well so he must be allowed to slow the tempo slightly to enable him to maintain the correct leg sequence and so a good rhythm. Should collection cause tension in the horse

Collected walk.

The two diagonals of the trot.

then it can result in him preferring to 'jog' rather than settle to the short walk. A long, relaxed outline is the only solution to this rather boring problem until sufficient relaxation is established.

TROT

This pace is the most popular for schooling purposes because of its two-time regular beat and so any changes to rhythm or tempo are easily felt by the rider. The rhythm of the trot is very important and it is because of the movement of this pace that such a variety of rhythm is seen. The trot strides are created by the horse bounding from one pair of diagonal legs to the other pair. In between each diagonal is a moment of suspension when all four feet are off the ground. The rhythm is, therefore affected by the size of the bound and the time taken through the moment of suspension. This is why a better rhythm is often produced by maintaining a slightly slower trot with a slightly longer period of suspension. The faster trot will tend to produce shorter, snappier steps and a quicker rhythm that is jarring and uncomfortable for the rider.

Collected Trot This is produced by the horse adopting a shorter outline and putting his energy into more elevated steps while remaining energetic and well engaged from behind. This trot is allowed to travel in a slightly slower rhythm and it is the job of the rider to maintain this rhythm and apply the leg and seat aids in time to it, so encouraging and assisting the horse to perform well. These elastic rhythmical steps can be broken by an unthinking rider applying a harsh or uncontrolled aid at the wrong moment.

Lengthened Trot When the trot strides are lengthened into medium or extension, again the rider must not interrupt the rhythm but sit still with poise and balance and encourage the horse with firm, calm aids. When performed correctly, the horse must be seen not only to lengthen the size of the strides but also the length of his outline while remaining on the bit. The increased engagement of the hind legs will enable the horse to take a bigger and longer bound forward. This will slightly increase the tempo but does not affect the rhythm which should show no appearance of going faster, only of taking bigger, longer strides to cover more ground. If the rider allows the horse to go faster and take quicker strides, it will only produce a tense running action, which is totally incorrect for lengthening.

It is sufficient for the novice to produce good lengthened strides in a balanced, rhythmical manner before he is asked to progress to either the medium or extended paces. It is only when the horse is approaching the medium level of work that the true extension is first asked for, and then only over short periods. It is, however, very important that the rhythm of these strides be maintained whether they be just lengthened or at full extension and over whatever distance.

CANTER

This is a three-time pace, followed by a moment of suspension. It is in this moment of suspension that the horse swings under and forward to the next stride. In this bound forward for the next stride the horse must travel forward approximately one whole length of his body. This action will produce a good working tempo. The rider must continue a commanding in-

---

Tempo

This is the speed with which every complete stride is taken and therefore the speed that the horse travels over the ground. To keep a good tempo the strides must be regular with each covering the same length of ground at the same speed.

Rhythm

This is created by the leg sequence within each of the strides and is the rhythm with which the feet are placed on the ground. Quite often the rider is more aware of rhythm and its quality in a two-time pace such as the trot than of the three-time rhythm of the canter. But whether it is a two-, three- or four-time rhythm he must learn to recognize its quality and be able to ride in rhythm with his horse, just as a dancer would move in rhythm to the music and with a partner.

fluence over the tempo and rhythm in the canter as in the other paces. This is achieved by the suppleness of his posture and his ability to swing his hips with the movement of the strides, so moving with the rhythm of the canter. The rider in this way will regulate the tempo of the canter and so develop the variants within the pace.

Working Canter This is the tempo most used as it is slow enough to assist the horse's balance in a restricted area yet energetic enough to keep a good stride and the correct leg sequence.

Collected Canter A shortening of the working tempo and a shortening of the outline will produce this. Performed correctly the horse must take more of his body-weight on the hind legs as they are engaged further under him. As in the trot, the tempo becomes a little slower and the rider will move in a slower rhythm to match that of the horse. If when shortened, the horse adopts a tense outline, both tempo and rhythm will then quicken, resulting in the canter becoming stilted in appearance with the front legs coming to the ground in a stiff, propping action. This action lacks any rhythm and prevents the rider from influencing the horse. Again, if the tempo at this

Right to left: the three steps of the canter followed by the moment of suspension: the outside hind leg comes to the ground; the diagonal pair come to the ground; the inside foreleg (leading leg) comes to the ground; the moment of suspension.

pace is slowed down too much, the true rhythm is lost and the horse adopts an incorrect leg sequence which produces a four-time beat instead of the three-time. Both these faults must be avoided to produce a true collected canter which, when well performed, is a delight to ride.

Lengthened Canter Again, as in the other paces, the horse must cover more ground by producing longer, enveloping strides, while retaining the same rhythm with the rider. If he is shortened, then again the strides will do the same and become shorter instead of longer.

It is the rider's conscientious efforts in all the paces that will establish their good rhythm. It must, nonetheless, be remembered that if the horse lacks good basic movement there will be limitations to the quality of his performance, however rhythmical the strides become.

Another contributing factor which can help enhance the movement and its rhythm, is the horse's ability to round in his outline. This will free the muscles over his back and in his shoulders, so giving a more elastic spring to the paces and an appearance of more extravagance.

The rider must again be reminded that the riding of the

paces through from collection to extension and back must be carried out in rhythm and must flow from one to another. They should not be taught or executed as individual movements that are totally unrelated, for all training must be interlinked and create a continual flow of energy.

SHORTENING AND LENGTHENING

Through regular balanced riding involving a variety of work, the novice horse will gradually take on a better outline with further muscular development over his top line. As this development is achieved, he will be more capable of lengthening and shortening his strides without interruption of rhythm and tempo.

Most of the regular work will have been carried out at a 'working' tempo and from this the horse must learn to make transitions into both collected and lengthened strides.

Shortening and lengthening. The more collected, shorter outline requires a shorter rein.

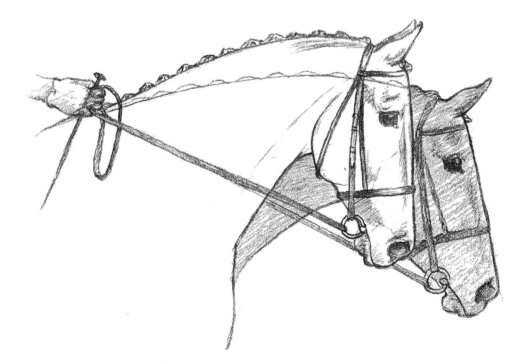

Shortening The job of shortening the horse will be assisted constantly by the use of half and full halts. These will help to bring the hind legs into a more engaged position under the body and enable them to take more of the body-weight. This attitude will gradually bring about the lightening of the fore-hand and subsequent ability to go in self-carriage. In these early stages changes will be only very slight but the rider will observe slight adaptations, with the horse more frequently being able to carry himself with a more raised head and neck carriage and without the loss of any roundness and sub-mission. This will enable him to adopt a position where he is

The changing outline from a lengthened to a more collected position.

travelling parallel to the ground with occasional lightening of the forehand, thus eliminating any tendency to fall on to the forehand (this should always be discouraged and will never improve the horse's balance).

Only when this stage has been reached is the horse ready to come into the correct shortened outline and work towards collection. The first action of shortening the outline is for the rider to shorten the reins. Although they are shortened they must not be strengthened as this would only result in a pulling action bringing the head back into the body rather than pushing the body up to the head. Once shortened, the reins must keep an easy, light contact with the mouth and their action should be to control the energy produced from the legs and seat.

This energy must then be guided by the appropriate feels being put on the reins. By the action of shortening the reins, the rider will shorten the horse's neck. This will require the horse to arch his neck more to accommodate himself in the shorter rein. This position must not be kept by force or strength but by the horse submitting to the feel of the bit in his mouth, and a light contact should be maintained with it. The rider must remember that the neck muscles will not be used to this extra flexion and so this position should be held initially only for short periods. These must be followed by short breaks which should allow the horse complete freedom of his neck, so relaxing the muscles before he is taken again into the shortened shape. By approaching the task in this way, and not being over-demanding, the horse should be prevented from fighting and evading the action of the shorter rein. With the action of the shorter rein and the intermittent use of the sitting trot to help stimulate the increased activity from behind, the horse will start to produce a correct shortened outline and, with the maintenance of rhythm and tempo, he will then produce balance and collection.

This same technique is used in all three paces but it is important to remember that in the walk the shortening must be kept to a minimum.

Lengthening The term lengthening means the progressive work advancing to medium and extended paces.

To lengthen the strides, the reins must be long enough to allow the head and neck to extend a little, but without loss of rein contact, as the slack or loose rein will not produce the desired effect. Should the rider try to keep a hand contact on too long a rein in the trot or at the canter, it can sometimes result in the rider lying back behind the movement in his efforts to maintain a contact. If this happens, the position and action will obviously discourage lengthening and often restrict and tense the horse in his performance. In fact, it produces the same result as a rider being left behind over a jump.

Some riders may find it easier to keep the same length of rein used for the general work and to allow the hands forward on a contact as the horse lengthens, returning to the original position after its execution.

With the novice, lengthening in the trot is usually more successful when carried out in the rising trot, provided the rider does not start to rise higher and faster as he asks for an increase in stride. A better form of lengthening will come from the controlled rider who stays low in his rising trot and maintains the same rhythm, with his leg aids used in that same rhythm.

With the naturally energetic horse, lengthening usually comes quite easily, with him being enthusiastic about providing extra energy for the strides. However, with the lazy type, the rider must play a more active role, doing all in his power to stimulate the activity required. With this type only ask for a few strides at a time until they are given freely with the horse being able to lengthen and shorten at will, like a piece of elastic. Once he understands the stimulating forces of the rider with extra use of seat, leg, voice and sometimes a little light use of the whip near the leg, he will respond more readily and make the task an easier one.

With some novice horses, the use of the canter can also help to stimulate the lengthened trot by frequent transitions between the two paces. Each time he is brought down into the trot, he must be encouraged to go straight into lengthened strides and then from the lengthened strides back into canter. These transitions can help a great deal in stimulating the trot. To carry out this exercise, the horse must be on good going; should he slip or lose his balance on bad going, it could destroy his confidence. Once these actions have stimulated an initial breakthrough and the horse starts to engage and lengthen, then more conventional aids and actions must be used.

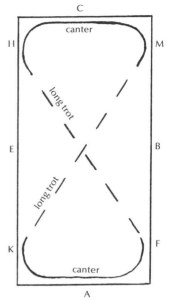

This exercise assists in lengthening the strides of the trot. Canter along the short sides and return to the lengthened trot on the diagonals.

Not all riders have the desire to compete, but probably the majority like the challenge of competition. Participation not only gives objectives and incentive to all the hard work, it also tests the rider's training and riding abilities – we can all have 'world champions' at home, it's proving it that is the test!

Competing requires a rider to have certain qualities that we do not all possess. However, novice tests are kept relatively simple and only require the horse to perform in a natural manner, showing purity of paces and balance to both left and right. Obedience to the aids are very important and to achieve this in a competition environment requires that the work at home has been extra thorough, as distractions on these occasions are numerous. For a rider to give a good account of himself at this level is not beyond the realms of most.

Once the horse is capable of a good novice performance, he should have started working towards elementary level at home. This is a good system to adopt throughout training, with the horse competing at a level lower than his training at home, making him confident and secure in his competition work.

Provided that the basic novice work has been well practised, the progression to elementary is not difficult. However, it is a very important one as it is the time when the horse must lose any tendency to fall on to the forehand as he must proceed into more collected work which requires a lightening of the forehand.

IMPROVING OUTLINE

The ability to work in a long outline with the head and neck extended must never be lost. It should be regularly practised but only when asked for by the rider. Often one sees horses left in this long outline with the rider thinking it is correct, resulting in the horse slipping on to his forehand when it can be difficult to get him off it. However, with correct use, it can create relaxation, lengthen and stretch muscles in the right places and lengthen strides; all very important. It is, therefore, best used for the warming up and finishing periods of training sessions, with the interim period being used for the practice of work associated with collection.

There is no sudden change in the horse at this stage and there will have been many times at the novice level when both

carriage and manner of going will have already been adequate for elementary level work. Now this must become a more regular happening with the horse doing this for longer periods and then through all paces.

Working in a long outline.

BEND

In producing a better outline many improvements will be necessary. One of these will be to improve the quality of bend, through tighter turns and smaller circles. The rider, through the action of his aids, must be able to increase or decrease bend as and when necessary. The first requirement of this is when the horse is ridden around the perimeter of the arena. 'Going large' requires the horse to be straight on the long and short sides and bent through the corners in the direction in which he is travelling. So far it has been sufficient to have only a slight curve to the horse as the track ridden has not demanded more. Gradually the horse must be asked to go deeper into each corner which will also require more bend. Each time a corner is ridden, a regular application of aids must be used to achieve this correctly with the horse learning that this particular use of the aids means that a corner is to be ridden.

Left: this horse and rider are in good balance on the canter half-circle. Right: this horse and rider are totally out of balance on the canter half-circle.

RIDING CORNERS AND TURNS

As a corner is approached the rider must apply the half halt. This will bring the horse to attention. The rider's inside leg must be firm in its application to maintain forward energy and to help keep the horse upright. The rider's outside leg is kept a little behind the girth to prevent any drift of the quarters to the outside. The inside hand asks for the head and neck to bend in the direction required by a light squeezing and giving action. The outside hand allows this bend but must maintain enough contact to control the speed through the corner. If the horse should show any tendency to fall in, then he can be helped into the upright by moving the outside rein a little away from the neck towards the corner. This must not be overdone as it could take the horse into the wrong bend, defeating the object of the exercise. The bend of the horse must match that of the curve being ridden with neither front nor back legs deviating from the line of the turn or curve. It is at this time that the horse is said to be straight through the turn.

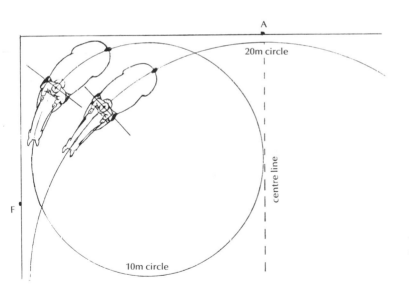

The difference in the curve through the corner between a novice and a more advanced horse.

Coming out of a corner on to the straight, the rider must prepare the horse by maintaining the outside rein contact and help him by the support of his inside leg to prevent him from continuing on to a circle.

The riding of circles, big or small, requires a similar technique and application of aids; the preparation for the circle and the finishing of it both require the same approach to return to the straight line. Bend to both directions should be equal so that no more strength is required on the left rein than is taken on the right, making turning and circling to both directions easy.

FLEXION

Flexion is the horse's ability to give in the top of his neck to the direction he is travelling. It is used on the straight and with bend.

To understand flexion, it is necessary to have a little understanding of equine anatomy. At the top of the cervical vertebrae of the neck is the axis bone. This fits into the atlas bone at the base of the skull. The joint between these two bones allows the head to hinge on the neck, both up and down and from left to right. Its downward hinging enables the horse to submit to the contact of the rein and its lateral hinging will give the flexion to left and right.

(a)   (b)

(a) An open space between head and neck for easy flexion; (b) a large jowl and glands closing the space makes flexion difficult.

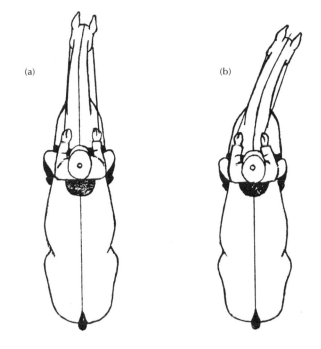

(a)   (b)

Lateral flexion is achieved by a light restraining and giving action on the inside rein and is used throughout work to both directions. When the direction changes, then so must the flexion, but the horse must be taken through the straight to the new flexion, never direct from one side to the other.

Flexion must be used in conjunction with bend and when the horse is on straight lines, he must be slightly flexed in the direction in which he is travelling or in the direction of the movement.

A horse with plenty of room through his gullet (the space between jowl and under-neck) will find flexion much easier than the horse with a shorter, thicker gullet and large glands in this area.

Flexion: (a) correct flexion is in the top third of the neck and does not involve bending through the body; (b) incorrect, exaggerated flexion.

EQUALITY AND STRAIGHTNESS

Crookedness in a horse is sometimes inherent and sometimes created by the rider. Although we can strive to sit square and equally across the horse, we are not always aware when we do not.

Left: this horse is cantering with quarters to the right. Right: this horse is cantering straightened.

Crookedness in a rider will create the appropriate counter-action from the horse, the result being that on the one hand the horse will probably lean in or out to bring his body under that of the rider or, on the other, will lean away from the direction of the rider's lean to counteract it.

Any deviations from the straight and upright must be corrected by the rider and are carried out by bringing the forehand in line with the quarters. The rider must not be tempted to move the quarters around in this situation as it will only create even greater problems, with the horse tending to swing them left and right when not required. One quite common fault in this respect is the horse that carries the quarters to the right, this being even more obvious when in canter right on a straight line. To bring the horse into the straight line, the aids must be applied, so if the forehand is on the desired riding line and the quarters have deviated to the right, then the rider must bring the forehand to the right and so bring it in line with the quarters. To achieve this the right rein must be taken a little to the right, while a steady contact is kept on the left with it pushed to the side of the neck. This action is assisted with the use of the outside leg on the girth to push the forehand over to the right. The inside leg maintains forward energy in its normal manner. Initially, these corrections are best carried out in walk when the horse has time to understand the aids clearly and the rider has time to apply them in the correct sequence.

Another cause of a crooked horse is also rider-related with the taking of a strong, constant feel down the inside rein, sometimes even pulling it to achieve either bend or direction. This will often result in the horse taking his quarters out and away from the direction required, so evading the bend asked for in this strong way. This must not only be corrected by moving the forehand but requires the rider to then keep a softer, more yielding action on the inside rein.

Equality to left and right is another contributing factor to progression not only in the horse's performance but the feel down the reins experienced by the rider. He must be increasingly aware of any resistances to either direction or of any inclination to take a stronger, deader feel on one rein.

If there is any stiffness to left or right more work on circles and turns to the stiff side will help to soften it. Combined with relaxation, resistances will be reduced and finally eliminated.

Should the feel experienced on one rein be considerably stronger and resistant, then light half halts must be applied repeatedly to that rein to lighten its contact and make it 'come alive'.

If the horse offers flexion in one direction more easily than in the other, then it can be discouraged by the rider keeping the horse straighter on his soft, easy side and then encouraging flexion to the stiff, resistant side, so making him more equal. The rider must constantly be aware of straightness and equality to left and right for without this all subsequent work will be incorrect.

As the horse's balance and physique develop he will be capable of carrying out a greater proportion of his work in collected paces. This outline will require him to take more weight on to the hind legs as they are more engaged under him. To engage in this manner and shorten and arch the neck to a higher position will complete the collected outline but will require that the horse's physique be well developed and the muscles on his top line strong. Only with this development will he be able to maintain the collection for any length of time.

It must be remembered that balance and lightness are not only improved through the horse's length where we observe the engagement of the quarters and the raising of the forehand, but it must also be observed in the upright, vertical position when viewed from the front or the back. This balance is increasingly important as the horse's education progresses and he is required to travel through tighter turns and circles. He will only be capable of this increased balance and lightness if his ability to stay in the vertical position also improves. This is greatly influenced by the rider and his ability to keep his body balanced above the horse. Any tendency to lean his weight in an uncontrolled way to one side or the other will encourage the horse to bring his body under the rider, resulting in both becoming unbalanced. Only when the centre line of the rider is over the centre line of the horse will true balance be maintained and the lightness of the forehand be improved. When this is achieved the horse will be capable of producing a more balanced, collected outline and because of this improved balance, he will be capable of executing it for longer periods.

Although he may be capable of lengthy periods in his outline, the rider must not spend the entire work programme expecting the horse to remain in this short position. There must be breaks where he allows the horse to stretch down and forward to relax him in this longer shape, so again putting him temporarily into the long novice position. In either position he should be capable of carrying himself on a light rein contact and must not lean on the bit or take support from the rider. It is only when the horse is returned to this longer shape that the rider can then ensure that he is working through from behind. This means the hind legs must produce both flexion and activity whilst being placed well under the body.

He must be certain that the arch so readily observed in the neck is, in fact, a roundness that starts with the engagement of the back legs and comes through the body and into the neck, so influencing the position and carriage of the head.

Horse and rider balanced in the vertical through a turn.

It is only necessary to use this longer outline for short periods and it can be of great help when warming up the horse

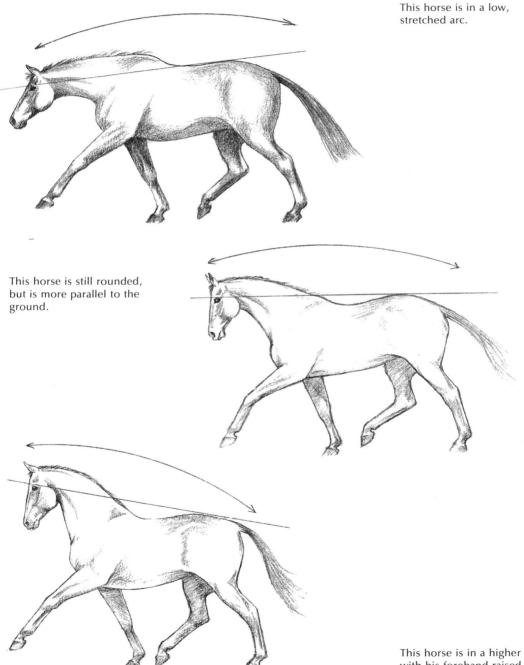

This horse is in a low, stretched arc.

This horse is still rounded, but is more parallel to the ground.

This horse is in a higher arc with his forehand raised.

and at the finish of a lesson to relax him. Then, in between, it can be used to punctuate the work sessions and so give relief from the concentrated work.

This collected outline enables the horse to be a responsive and balanced ride and carry out all the work so far covered in a light and energetic way. The rider should feel a change in the horse with this progression and will find him lighter in the hand and more responsive to the aids and supple through his back, so making him very comfortable to ride. At this time the rider should experience a new dimension to his riding when he feels totally at one with the horse and is able to control him with the lightest of aids. These moments of pleasure are, at first, short-lived but with further training and improved balance, they become more frequent and part of the everyday riding programme.

It is not sufficient to train a horse to a level, whether it be novice or advanced and think that the task is finished. It is true that any work correctly carried out in a horse's life will not be forgotten but to sustain or to improve on that work, there must be regular, sometimes even daily practice to achieve greater things. Only then will muscles, tendons and ligaments be kept supple and healthy and able to perform at their best.

VARIETY OF WORK

The horse destined for a career in dressage does not have to spend his entire time schooling and practising. He can be taught to jump, cross country or do anything that might be pleasurable for him and for his rider.

In normal circumstances this improves the horse's outlook on life and he will then return to his job fresh and attentive. However, occasionally one comes across a horse that only improves his dressage when he works at it daily and finds it difficult to perform after a day off. Remember they are all individuals and it is not possible to generalize and put all horses in the same class.

Throughout training, at whatever level, the quality of the work is of the utmost importance and not the quantity or the speed at which it is done. As much pleasure will be gained from a simple task really well performed as the riding of more advanced movements involving a highly schooled horse.

HEAD CARRIAGE

As the horse progresses from novice to more advanced levels and is able to arch his neck more and give in the poll, so the angle of the head to the neck becomes greater when the front of the face comes more into the vertical position. It must be remembered that this position *must* be produced by the engagement from the hind legs and *not* by pulling and restraining the reins to bring the head back into the neck. When the horse resists the feel from the hands and either 'pokes' his nose or yanks forward and leans on the bit, the rider must try to remedy this by activating the driving aids to push the horse up to the bit contact, so momentarily increasing the weight in the hand. In this moment, the horse should submit to this stronger contact and the rider must then yield with the hand as a reward.

OVER-BENDING

Care must be taken not to over-bend the horse in the neck, so getting the head position behind the vertical. When this happens the rider will lack control as the horse learns that in this position he can evade the rider's hand aids by tucking back into his neck and often either dropping the bit contact or leaning heavily on it. The rider must recognize when enough flexion is achieved and not go on asking for more but lighten the contact instead. So often we see riders over-using hand and rein aids and literally pulling the head towards the neck, putting the horse into a very uncomfortable position from which he will fight to escape. This is not good riding and should never be practised.

REIN CONTACT

The maintenance of a good rein contact becomes increasingly important. No two riders exert the same contact down a rein; it is an individual feel gradually developed between horse and rider, and one that the rider must use as frequently as possible. With this regular, easy contact from the rider, the horse will learn to be confident in his work and submit easily to the

Head positions.

rider's wishes. Should the rider always use strength or force in his rein contact, the horse will think that this is the norm and always expect it before he will respond to the aids. Different horses will accept different contacts. One horse might have a very sensitive mouth and will always need to be ridden on a light contact, whereas another might have a much more solid feel to the mouth when the rider might have to keep a much more animated feel from the fingers to keep the contact 'alive' and so initiate the same response from the horse.

Only with this acceptance of the rein contact will it be possible to work the horse to a shortened rein, then into a shortened outline and finally into collection.

This horse is working on a shorter rein with a raised head and neck.

The influence of collection in the work programme will greatly enhance its quality and make turns, circles and so on, far more balanced. Once in better balance, the transitions can be improved through the paces and, as the responses to the aids improve, they can then be more direct in their execution.

Working (on the bit) will become easier for the horse with practice, as the top muscles become capable of coping with the increased flexion and stretching. He will then be able to work for longer periods in this position provided it is interspersed with periods of walk on a free rein.

With the improvement of physique and balance, the rider will be able to develop and to improve rein contact. This is only possible as the horse's physique develops and strengthens so enabling him to carry himself with better carriage and balance. At this time the contact down the rein (from hand to mouth) must be developed and improved to produce a light, elastic feel of soft submission. It should not consist of strength, lean, excessive weight or resistances as with these poor qualities the responses between horse and rider will lack finesse.

To develop this refined feel, the horse must be engaged forward from the driving aids into the contact offered from the hands. This contact must not discourage the horse by any backwards feel being taken with the hands. They should offer a steady feel that must yield to the horse when he adopts light carriage on the reins.

THE YIELDING REIN

The rider must occasionally test this quality by giving the reins forward either as a pair or individually when the horse must seek forward a little with the head and neck but in no way must he take a dive for their support when the contact of the hands has gone, so falling on to his forehand.

The soft submissive feel received by the hand is produced when the horse relaxes in his lower jaw and flexes in his poll. This flexing is produced by the vertical hinging action between the axis and atlas bones at the top of the neck and allows the horse to adopt the correct position with the head while the poll stays at the highest point. When a horse is capable of this head carriage while remaining engaged from behind, he is said to be 'on the bit'.

At this stage the rider can introduce the horse to the 'lateral aids' – those that push him sideways as well as forward. The rider will feel a sense of achievement having reached this stage and it will give another dimension to his riding.

Before attempting any movements involving sideways steps, the rider must be fully aware of the requirements and objectives that are relative to each movement.

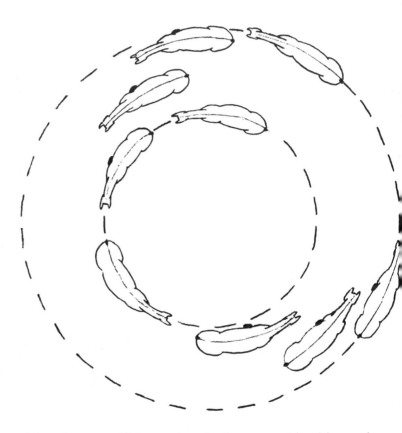

The leg yield. The horse is taken from the 20m circle to the 10m circle and then is taken back to the 20m circle in leg yield.

Most horses will have already done considerable work on circles and turns. This work will have introduced them to the effect achieved from a strong inside leg and its action of preventing the horse from falling to the inside. If the action of this leg is increased still more, it is possible to make the horse move away from this active leg and take his first steps sideways. This can be instigated from the 20m circle. First, the circle must be reduced to approximately 10–12m, then the rider increases the action of the inside leg on the girth and pushes the horse out sideways, back to the large circle. This push from the inside leg must be helped by the action of the outside rein leading the horse away to the large circle. The inside rein is taken to the neck to assist this action and must, at the same time, maintain the bend to the inside.

The rider's position in the saddle can also prove helpful. By putting more weight to the inside seat bone it will assist the action of leg and hands. However, the rider must take care in

The rider is pushing the horse off the right leg out to the large circle.

this situation not to drop his inside shoulder down towards his inside hip as this would cause a lack of balance to the position and is a bad habit difficult to correct. This simple sideways movement from small to large circle must be practised to both reins, so keeping the horse equal in both directions. It is important in these first sideways movements to supple the horse equally, making him easily manoeuvrable to left and right.

These movements will add interest and increased variety to schooling sessions and will require both horse and rider to be balanced and responsive. All sideways steps necessitate greater activity from behind as the horse is required to move the inside leg up and over the outside one, causing greater development and strengthening in the quarters.

TURN ON THE FOREHAND

In this turn the hind legs must tread a circle around the fore-legs, the horse moving his body away from the rider's outside leg.

The horse must halt parallel to the long side of the arena but well to the inside of the track to allow him room to turn. Take feel on the outside rein to flex the horse to this direction, move the leg on the same side behind the girth and with a driving action push the quarters away to the opposite direction. As the horse produces each step, the rider must pause with his driving leg aid. The opposite rein must prevent the horse from stepping forward and also stop the horse turning too much to the bend asked for with the outside rein. The inside leg will remain on the girth and discourage any backward steps.

These aids must ask the horse to complete a 180° turn, then he will be facing in the opposite direction and can proceed forward. The leg aids applied for this turn will necessitate the horse to move his body away from their driving action and so develop his ability to step sideways.

HALF PIROUETTE

This movement requires the horse to turn within his own length through 180° so he is facing in the opposite direction. At this stage of training it is performed from the walk and 3–4

teps should be taken for its execution. Later on in his career, it vill also be performed in canter and can then include the full urn of 360° within the horse's own length.

The turn requires the moving of the forehand around the uarters, the front legs describing a large half-circle and the ind legs a small one, the inside hind leg treading up and down lmost on the spot. Initially, the turn is best performed along ie long side of the school and can be started from the halt, vhen it is called the 'turn of the haunches' or from the walk, vhen it is called the 'half pirouette'.

Should the horse try to rush into the turn or ignore the side-vays requests of the aids by marching off forward, it would be etter performed from the halt when each step can be ex-lained and controlled. Should the horse show the opposite endencies and try to creep backwards, then it would be better aught and performed from walk to keep the activity behind.

The horse must first be flexed to the direction of the turn and ien the forehand must take the first step to the side. This is

Anti-clockwise from top right: a horse executing a half pirouette.

Correct

Incorrect

The half pirouette. The turn is on the haunches with the inside foot treading a small circle. If the quarters 'pop out' away from the turn, then the turn is on the centre and not on the haunches.

done by the inside rein leading it to the inside of the track while the outside rein regulates the amount of movement and direction taken by the inside. This first stride of the turn should place the horse into the same position as that required to perform the shoulder-in, the same aids then being repeated with every subsequent step. As the feels are put on the reins, care must be taken that the horse does not step backwards; to prevent this, the forward driving action from the legs must not be lost. Once the turn has started, the rider's outside leg initially must provide assistance in moving the horse to the inside and then, by moving it back behind the girth, its activity will prevent the quarters from popping out away from the turn. This evasion would then change it to a turn on the centre with the forehand going to one direction and the quarters going to the other.

Following the full 180° turn the horse must continue the fluent forward movement along the track, when he must be positioned into the new inside bend. The rider must keep his weight to the inside seat bone with a long inside leg. Care must be taken by the rider in this position that he does not collapse to the inside by dropping the inside shoulder towards the hip. This faulty position would then drive the horse's quarters away from the turn, so causing it to be totally incorrect.

Performing the pirouette can be of great benefit to the training programme by assisting in the collection of the horse, with increased activity and engagement of the hind legs, so lightening the forehand. It can also stimulate the responses to the rider when executed following the trot or canter. First the rider must cease the trot or canter, walk a few steps, perform the half turn from the walk, take the new bend and proceed again into the trot or canter. Once the horse realizes the requirements of these exercises, he will respond far more readily to the aids and their actions, so again assisting in the creation of collection.

LEG YIELD

The use of the leg yield can be beneficial in teaching the horse to move off the rider's inside leg and can help as a forerunner to shoulder-in. The requirements of the movement are that the horse should move forward and sideways while giving very slight bend away from the direction in which he is travelling.

The leg yield: (a) the horse is turned to the three-quarter line and the inside leg is applied to drive him out to the left; (b) the next progression is to perform the movement down the long side of the arena.

One benefit is that it teaches the horse to move forward and sideways away from the inside leg, so encouraging the action of moving the inside legs over and across the outside legs.

It is felt by some that this movement can cause confusion to the horse in that it is similar to teaching him a half pass but with the wrong bend, therefore reasoning it is wrong to teach him an incorrect action and then expect him to relearn it correctly. To decide whether or not to use the leg yield is, I think, dependent on the individual horse and his responses to the rider.

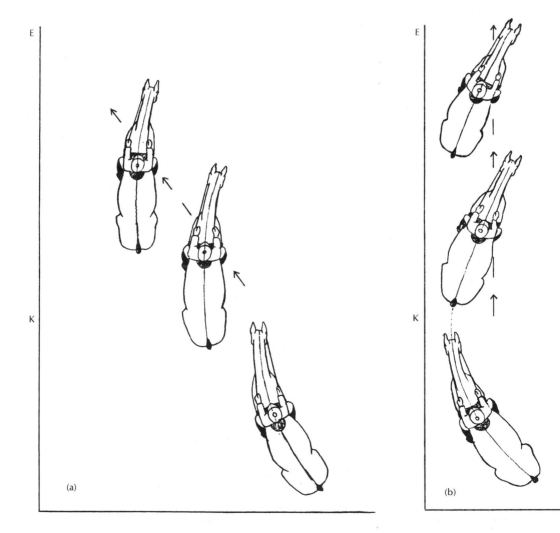

With the active athletic type who is always willing to try, it might be better to move straight into shoulder-in and then half pass. With the rather lazy, heavy type, it might be beneficial to make him a bit sharper off the leg and so encourage more instant responses.

The leg yield is best performed in walk but again, with some, can be more stimulating if performed for short periods in trot. The easiest way to start the movement is from the three-quarter line back to the long side of the school. If the horse is being ridden to the right rein he is turned to the three-quarter line, (approximately 5m from the track), instead of being turned on to the centre line. While a slight right bend is maintained, the inside (right) leg on the girth will drive the horse out to the left and on to the track. He must remain almost parallel to the long side, having to step both forward and sideways as he travels diagonally back to the track. The rider must encourage activity so that the horse's inside legs step over and across the outside legs, with a swinging action.

The next progression is to perform the movement down the long side of the arena where the horse is positioned with his shoulders to the inside of the track at an angle of approximately 10°–45°. Once in this position, the bend is maintained into the arena while the inside leg drives the horse down the track. Initially, this is more easily carried out in the walk and will teach the horse to move off the inside leg. When in this position it will make the horse cross inside legs over outside ones, having the effect of opening up the shoulder movement. This can only be achieved if the correct angle is maintained in a constant manner throughout the exercise.

Once the horse is proficient to both directions, his responses can be tested further by being asked to leg yield from the long side into 'X' and back to the long side before the corner is reached. This is performed from the corner on to the long side. While being kept parallel to the track, he is taken into the outside bend and with drive from the leg on that side, he is pushed into the arena towards 'X'. Just before 'X' he is made straight and kept parallel to the long side. He is then taken into the opposite bend and, with the opposite leg the rider drives him back to the track before the end of the long side.

Once this can be achieved in a co-operative manner, the horse will have a thorough understanding of moving away

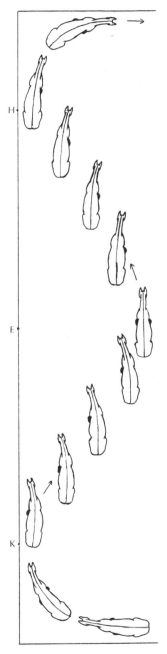

The leg yield from the long side into the X and back again.

(Left to right) Shoulder-in.

from the driving leg on the girth. This exercise will also help the rider to bend the horse by being able to ride him from inside leg into outside rein. Another way it can help schooling is if there should ever be a problem achieving a canter lead. At the time when the horse is pushed back to the track he is then in an ideal position for the canter transition to the direction of that bend.

SHOULDER-IN

The shoulder-in is probably the most important and useful lateral movement available to the rider. It requires the horse to be placed at an angle of approximately 30° to the line being ridden. The shoulders are moved to the inside of that line and the hind legs kept on it, so producing three tracks: the inside foreleg produces the first track; the inside hind leg and outside foreleg the second; and the outside hind leg the third track. Once in this position, the horse must remain bent to this direction and move off the rider's inside leg. By this action, the

activity of the hind legs will be greatly improved, especially the inside leg. The leg action of the horse will be for the inside hind leg to step over and in front of the outside leg and for the inside foreleg to repeat this action over the outside foreleg. This will develop the up and under action from the inside hind leg and it also helps to open the shoulders and give more freedom to the front legs.

Once the rider is able to manoeuvre the horse's shoulders to where he requires them, it will assist him in the straightening of the horse throughout all his work. When in position for shoulder-in, the horse must not be allowed to evade the movement by swinging his quarters away to the outside of the line being ridden. The maintenance of activity and tempo is very important throughout its execution, when regularity of the length and rhythm of the steps must be maintained from start to finish.

The first attempts at shoulder-in can be asked for on the circle. This gives the rider time to explain the requirements to his mount without running out of room. As an introduction to this work, the horse can be asked to increase the inside bend of head and neck to the inside of the circle, while his body is

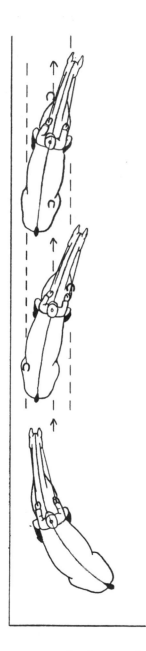

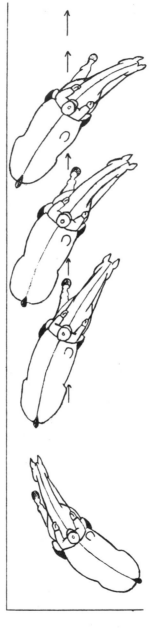

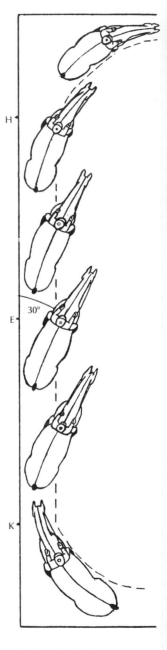

Positioning for the start of the shoulder-in.

A common fault in the shoulder-in – the horse turns and bends his neck too much into the arena.

A shoulder-in down the long side of the arena at a 30° angle to the wall.

kept to the perimeter line of that circle. This is best attempted from an active trot and every effort must be made to maintain this forward energy while positioning him. Following this, the rider can then attempt the shoulder-in position which is achieved by the rider taking the head, neck and shoulders slightly into the circle. As this position is taken, the rider must increase the drive from his inside leg to maintain impulsion and the position of the shoulders. The outside hand will regulate and control the amount of position taken by the inside hand and the energy produced by the inside leg. The outside leg will stop the quarters deviating from the circle. Once the horse understands what is required, the feel on the inside rein can intermittently be yielded to allow the horse to remain lightly in position.

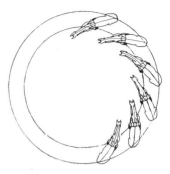

A shoulder-in on a large circle. The hind legs are kept on the perimeter line while the forelegs are taken in to the inside.

When a reasonable response is achieved on the circle, then attempts can be made from the straight line. The long side of the arena is best for this effort and will be assisted if there is a perimeter fence of some sort as this will help to discourage any tendency for the quarters to deviate from the ridden line. In the first instances, do not expect too much from the horse. Any slight willingness to respond to the aids must be praised in order to encourage further attempts. Particular attention must be paid to placing the horse at the correct angle to the track and maintaining it through as much of the movement as possible. Should it be lost temporarily and attempts to reposition fail, then he must be taken on to a small (10m) circle and, on returning to the track, repositioned for the shoulder-in. Once this angle and impulsion can be maintained over the desired length, then bend and flexion must also be kept to produce the correctness for this movement.

This correct performance can assist and improve other movements, one of these being the trot and the extension of that pace. Increased bend and activity of the hind legs will engage them more efficiently which will then allow more freedom through the shoulders, so producing more action and extravagance at this pace.

The shoulder-in position can also enhance the quality of the half pass by placing the horse correctly for its start, eliminating any tendency to begin the movement with the quarters leading. Being able to position the shoulders plays an important role throughout training and will prove invaluable in the education and production of the dressage horse.

TRUE CANTER AND TRANSITIONS

The canter must be developed to the same degree as the other paces. In fact, as schooling progresses, the canter plays a more important role by its more frequent use and the increased number of movements performed in it. To proceed even further into counter canter, it is necessary for the true canter to be both well performed and balanced. Equally, once the horse is able to work in counter canter, it will help to improve the balance of the true canter.

From the working canter, the rider must aim towards collecting the horse into a shorter outline. This is achieved by greater engagement of the hind legs, bringing them further under him and so taking a greater portion of his weight. This engagement is stimulated by the driving aids, but at the same time it must not produce greater speed. The energy produced will create a higher bound to the stride, which if controlled on the shorter rein, will put the horse into a higher neck and head carriage. At this time, the strength down the rein must not increase but the horse must stay round and submissive in his attitude. The collected canter will produce better balance and allow the horse to be more manoeuvrable within the arena.

Changes of direction and, at the same time, changes of

Left to right: The transition down from canter right through the walk and into canter left.

leading leg, will require the horse to be proficient through the transition. With the novice these are first performed through trot, but once working in more collection they must also be performed through walk. The walk to canter and canter to walk transitions become easy once fully understood and well practised. The easier of these is the step from walk into canter and at first is best performed from the small (10m) circle. The rider must be aware of the aid requirements for this transition. He must shorten the reins to collect the walk around the small circle, the inside leg must maintain its normal driving action on the girth, the inside rein must ask for and maintain the bend, and the outside rein must control the bend taken to the inside and discourage any increase of tempo at the walk. The outside leg is taken behind the girth and applied firmly to ask for the canter transition, assisted by drive from the rider's seat in the saddle. The sequence of aids for this transition must be: shorten reins, collect walk, take inside bend, inside leg on girth, outside leg behind girth, seat and leg aids to urge horse into canter. When this transition is asked for from the small circle, the aids must start their application about three-quarters of the way round the circle, thus the canter is given as the circle is finished and the horse is then allowed forward on the larger circle.

Canter to walk. The rider is bracing her back to assist the transition.

The transition from canter back into walk will need more practice for its correct execution and will require the rider to maintain control of his own balance and position. It is not sufficient for him just to pull on the reins as this action will only pull the horse's head into his body, overbending his neck and encouraging him to surge on to his forehand. This will result in an unbalanced and progressive transition which is totally opposite to the requirements.

Performed correctly, the horse must first be well engaged from behind, so allowing the forehand to remain light. Any increase in speed will only hinder the transition and must be discouraged. The rider must feel the swing under of the hind legs and must encourage this energy through the horse into his reins and hands which must then block any further progress in canter and place the horse down into walk. The rider must assist these actions through his body posture by adopting a braced back and a deep seat to give support to the restraint on the reins. His legs at this time remain on the horse to encourage the steps forward to walk following the transition.

In its initial execution this transition is best performed after only a short time in canter (approximately half a 20m circle) as the horse will then still be light on his forehand. The longer the canter continues, the more difficult the task becomes as, with a comparative novice, he will tend to slip gradually on to his forehand and then only be capable of the heavy and progressive transition to walk. Once he fully understands the restraining and arresting action of the rider's aids and is able to remain balanced, this transition will become as easy as the upward one.

To improve the canter the horse must be well engaged and in a rounded outline.

When the horse is able to canter in balance and collection, he can gradually be introduced to the counter canter. This means that once engaged in canter to a leading leg, the direction of riding can be changed without changing the leading leg. It requires the horse to remain in bend and balance to the leading leg and is initially only practised for a few strides on a straight line.

FIRST EXERCISES

The simplest method of executing this is to proceed in canter down the long side of the school and, at the end of the long side, take the horse on to a half-circle – approximately 10m – and return to the long side to change the direction. As he comes to the track, the rider must keep him flexed and slightly bent to his leading leg (now on the outside) and ask him to continue down the long side in this canter for a few strides before being brought back to trot or walk. In this exercise the horse must not be taken too close to the edge of the arena but kept to an inner track. This is because he will need a little more room to enable him to stay in the canter while bent to the outside. If this is not allowed he might feel restricted and so get tense and break from the canter.

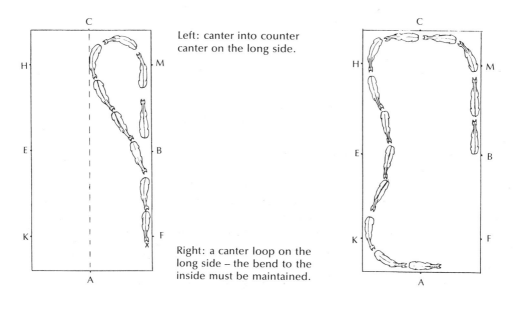

Left: canter into counter canter on the long side.

Right: a canter loop on the long side – the bend to the inside must be maintained.

RIDER'S AIDS DURING COUNTER CANTER

When he can maintain his balance and keep the canter for short periods like this, he can then proceed to the next stage of cantering through the half-circle while remaining on the outside lead. There are no special aids for counter canter, only that the rider should apply the aids in a very positive manner while remaining in the same balance. The rider should not shift his weight or pull a rein to the new direction as this will only upset the horse's balance and make him break from his stride or attempt to change legs in the canter. Should this happen he must be taken back to perform the movement again. However, the rider must realize that most problems with this exercise normally lie with him rather than with the horse.

Counter canter. The horse must remain bent to the left lead and the rider must also sit in the same balance.

COUNTER CANTER THROUGH HALF-CIRCLES

When first asked to continue the counter canter through the half-circle, the horse must be allowed to take a shallower arc that will not prove too testing for him so keeping well out of the corners and rather flattening the shape. The rider must maintain the same bend and balance as he had in the true canter and ask for it with the same aids. Once into the counter canter, the rider must maintain or even increase the forward drive to encourage the horse through this period and so encourage him to keep in the canter stride.

The rider's outside leg and inside rein must play an important and influential role by their firmer application, so preventing the horse from changing his position and adopting a new bend.

The work in counter canter can improve the horse's balance at this pace, bringing him more into the upright to whichever direction he travels, so helping to keep him straight through his body and avoiding any tendency to swing the quarters to left or right. For correct execution at more advanced levels, the horse will be required to describe serpentines consisting of 10m half-circles to true and counter canter, proving he can remain totally in a balanced and upright position. It will also be used in the preparatory work for the flying change when he must become totally obedient to the aids, staying in counter canter until the aid is applied to perform the flying change.

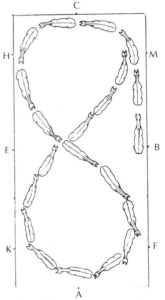

When the counter canter is continued through the full half-circle, the line must be kept as simple and easy as possible by flattening the corners and keeping well away from the wall. To finish, return to a true canter across the diagonal.

If the first sideways steps are well learnt and practised, the horse will have a true understanding of moving away from the rider's leg aids, while still maintaining balance in all his basic work. He must now increase his responses to the rider's aids, so becoming more supple and manoeuvrable to both directions, giving readily to the actions of the legs. So at this time we can introduce the more demanding lateral work of *renvers*, *travers* and *half pass*.

RENVERS

In the renvers the horse is placed in a shoulder-in position but this time, instead of being bent to the inside and away from the direction being travelled (as in a true shoulder-in), his body is

Above: a renvers on the long side of the arena.

Right: renvers. The same angle as shoulder-in but with the opposite bend.

positioned at the same angle – approximately 30° to the long side – and is now bent to the outside and towards the direction in which he is travelling. He must at this time keep his hind legs on the track – the inside legs will cross over and in front of the outside ones.

To start the renvers from the long side of the school, the rider must take the forehand to the inside of the track with both reins. The inside rein will ask for this position and maintain it. The outside rein will ask for bend to the outside and to the direction being travelled. The rider's inside leg will be taken behind the girth and in this position drive the horse down the track, while the outside leg stays on the girth and keeps the horse up to the bit, so discouraging any backwards steps while supporting the bend asked for by the outside rein.

Alternating between shoulder-in and renvers is a good exercise for the horse and he must respond readily to the change of bend while maintaining the same angle and position to the long side of the arena. Another test of the horse's obedience is to perform the shoulder-in and then ask the horse for the turn on the haunches in the corner at the end of the long side (the shoulder-in position making the first stride of the turn). Instead of completing the turn and making the horse change to the new bend, the turn is finished one stride from the track, the position and the bend maintained, and while holding these the horse is pushed with the new inside leg down the track in renvers.

These exercises are demanding for the horse and must not be overdone until the horse is physically strong enough to cope with them and shows no stress in the effort needed. They can be quite stimulating for the slow and inactive horse as they ask for a variety of movements over a short time. If the shoulder-in is performed in trot, the horse should be asked to walk for one or two strides, put into the turn on the haunches and then, from this turn, put straight back into trot for the renvers.

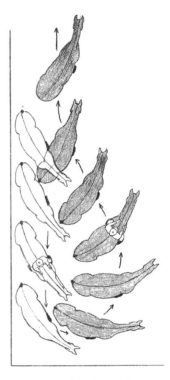

A shoulder-in up the long side of the arena followed by a half pirouette in the corner and a return down the long side in renvers. The driving leg changes from inside to outside during the movement.

TRAVERS

The travers is another two-track movement used to teach the horse to travel sideways and forward and involves him crossing his outside pair of legs over and across the inside pair.

Left to right: travers. The quarters are inside the track and the horse is bent to the direction in which he is travelling.

Through the movement the forehand is kept to the track while the quarters are moved to the inside, again creating an angle of approximately 30°. Although performed usually on the long side of the school, it can also be practised on a circle, with the quarters being placed to the inside. A good exercise on a circle is to alternate between shoulder-in and travers, so truly controlling both forehand and quarters.

In the travers the bend through the horse must be kept to the direction being travelled and is produced with feel on the inside rein. The outside rein will help to control the shoulders and stop them deviating from the track by its firm application, but not to the extent that it takes the bend to the outside. The inside leg must be applied to the girth where it has two actions: one of helping to keep the bend and the other of keeping the horse forward to the bit. The outside leg must take an active role and hold and drive the quarters down the inside of the track, maintaining their position throughout the movement.

It is felt by some trainers that teaching the travers can have an adverse affect on the straightening of the horse by him being asked to carry his quarters in. However, others feel that

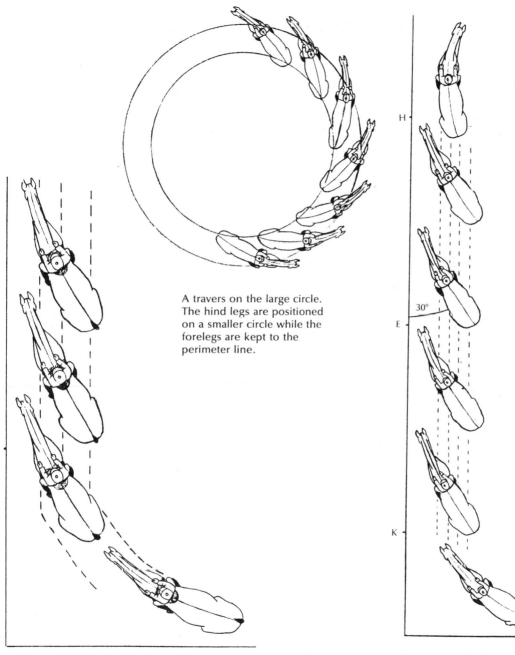

A travers on the large circle. The hind legs are positioned on a smaller circle while the forelegs are kept to the perimeter line.

Preparing for the start of the travers.

A travers on the long side of the arena at an angle of 30° to the wall.

with the correctly schooled horse it should be possible for the rider to position the horse both how and where he wants him without the horse learning it as a bad habit.

HALF PASS

Once the horse is responsive to the initial two-track movements, progression to the half pass should prove relatively straightforward. However, if the aids become too complicated or the task made too difficult early on, it can cause the horse to become tense in his attempts and spoil its correct execution.

The half pass is normally performed from the centre line back to the long side of the arena. Correctly performed, the horse

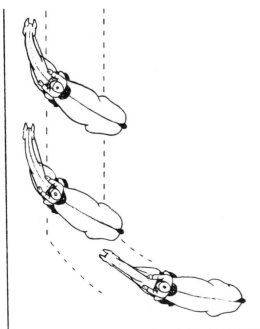

An incorrect travers results if the neck is over-bent laterally and the body left straight.

Half pass. The horse and rider are in balance with the horse in correct bend and with its forehand slightly leading.

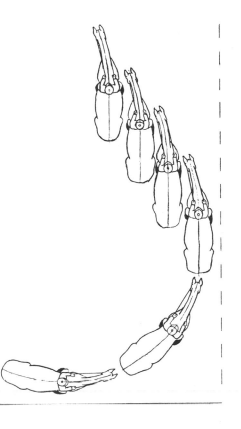

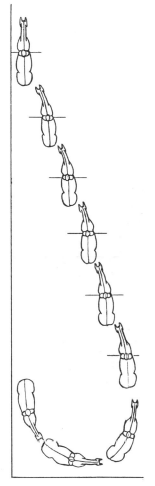

Left: a correct half pass from the centre line back to the long side.

must be taken to the centre line while maintaining the bend of the turn. The horse must then be kept in this bend throughout the movement. The direction of this movement is along a diagonal line. The horse's body position along that line is one that keeps him almost parallel to the long side of the arena but with his forehand slightly preceding his quarters. In this position and direction he can travel both forwards and sideways back to the track with outside foreleg and hind leg crossing over and in front of the inside legs.

Putting the horse into position for the start of the half pass is most important. Should there be any tendency for him to lead with the quarters, he must be corrected by being put into the shoulder-in position on the centre line. This will ensure that the shoulders move into the half pass fractionally ahead of the quarters. Another problem at the start of this movement occurs if the rider thinks only of going sideways and so forgets

Make the most of the arena length when you practise the half pass in order to give the horse every opportunity to perform the movement correctly.

The horse and rider are in the upright position. The horse is bent to the left for a left half pass and the rider has her left leg fractionally lower than her right leg.

the forwards movement. This urgent need of the rider to go sideways can result in the horse rushing off back to the side of the arena, often in the wrong bend and so lacking the necessary parallel position for the correct execution of the movement.

The aids for the half pass must be kept uncomplicated and simple in their application. From the turn to the centre line, the inside rein will maintain the bend of that turn and direct the horse into the half pass. The outside rein controls the amount of bend and positions the shoulders throughout the movement. The inside leg must be used on the girth to maintain the forward movement and the bend; the outside leg moves behind the girth to activate the sideways drive of the horse.

The rider's body posture is very important and should not be twisted to the direction of the movement but kept at right angles to the long side of the arena. Only in this position will it be possible to keep sufficient control over the forehand and maintain its correct position relative to that of the quarters. The rider's weight in the saddle must be kept into the direction of the half pass and this is assisted by the rider stretching down his inside leg in order to maintain his balance with the horse.

Half pass. The horse and rider are out of balance with the horse trying to rush off to the side of the arena.

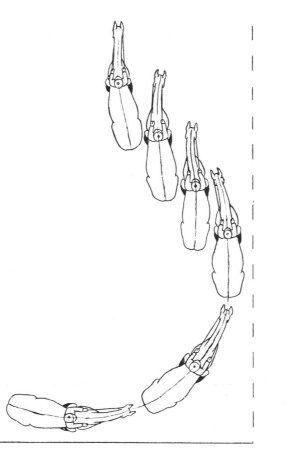

The half pass. In this case the movement starts off correctly, but then the horse falls on his inside shoulder resulting in him going on the wrong bend at the end.

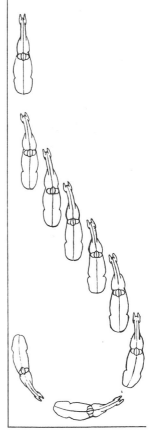

The energy and activity of the horse throughout the half pass must be stimulated and maintained by the rider, and his actions of bending and directing the horse sideways must not destroy this desire to step forwards.

Once the horse is truly moving with energy through the half pass, he can be asked to make steeper traverses across the full width of the school, requiring him to step forwards and sideways with extravagance. This should not be attempted too early in his education as it will prove too demanding. This could cause tension and so limit the amount of crossing he produces. The half pass executed correctly, with gymnastic strides, is an exciting movement to watch and demonstrates true co-ordination of energy and movement by both horse and rider.

The half pass. This line is too steep back towards the track and will prove difficult in the early stages.

As training progresses we will see the development of true harmony between horse and rider, enhancing performance and enabling even greater co-operation to develop. To assist this development the rider must practise and be capable of greater powers of concentration, and have the desire and dedication to hard work that is only seen in a minority of riders. Only when possessing these qualities is it possible to demand greater mental and physical efforts from the horse.

Once the horse is capable of performing a number of medium movements in a straightforward manner, it is time for the rider to think forward to the next level of work. First, the quality of the work already learned must improve so as to make further advances, improving and extending the horse's ability. In his lateral work he must flow from one movement to another in a supple manner, showing no resistance to the aids of his rider. The quality of the half pass must be developed further and its degree of difficulty gradually increased. This will require the horse to travel through a steeper angle and to traverse the full width of the arena. At this time he can also be taught the counter changes of hand which require him to perform a zig-zag pattern through the length of the arena. These changes of direction will ask the horse to reposition himself quickly each time, without interrupting the flow of energy or causing him to fall or lose balance as the direction is changed. This will require a greater suppleness through his body and only when this is achieved will he be capable of equal length of steps to both left and right.

During the improvement of the half pass in trot, the rider can also introduce him to the canter half pass. To perform this well he must be capable of a balanced and collected canter which will enable him to hold both position and bend while travelling forwards and sideways through the movement. Once these qualities can be maintained, the half pass in canter is no more difficult to perform than in the trot, and only requires the rider to apply the aids in the same manner.

With this further development of individual movements, the improvement of the horse's general outline, involving his suppleness and elasticity, must not be neglected. This will also necessitate the horse being able to flow from collected paces to extension with ease, showing no excessive effort from the rider. At all times he must stay in a rounded outline as only then will he remain engaged from behind, making him lighter in the hand.

As more demanding work with collection is asked for and maintained for longer periods, the rider must not neglect the periods of relaxation and the walk. In these periods the horse will be allowed complete freedom to stretch and extend through his whole length and so improve the walk steps.

With this improved standard of work the rider will increasingly find that he has much better control over the horse. This control will enable him to place and position both forehand and quarters where he requires them and enable him to raise and lighten the forehand and position it to left or right as required. He will be able to lower and engage the quarters and again place them in either direction as required. Lastly, he will be able to lengthen or shorten the complete outline, so producing extension and collection. Only with this degree of control is it possible for the rider to place the horse in the correct position, so enabling him to perform all movements with maximum balance and ease.

As that work becomes well established, the rider is then on the threshold of advanced work, which can prove a very exciting time when the rewards of many hours of work can be enjoyed. Unfortunately, some horses, however obedient and well trained, do not possess the physical capabilities to make them top horses. Every horse has limitations, which can involve either gymnastic ability or temperament, but either will limit the level of achievement. This does not detract in any way from the personal sense of achievement experienced by the rider in training a horse to this level or from the enjoyment it can give to the individual. In fact, training a limited or mediocre horse to these higher levels can often require greater skill from the rider than carrying out the same job with a naturally talented horse. When involved in the training of such a talented horse, an average rider can be made to look very impressive.

There are a number of factors which contribute to producing the dressage horse and which can either make the job easy or more complicated.

Temperament This is probably the most important influence in the training programme. Good temperament will produce a co-operative horse, allowing the work to advance with ease and in an uncomplicated manner. In a less obliging horse, it can result in many hours being spent overcoming basic resistance and the rider will find that only limited advances are made.

Exaggerated Movement This can be very advantageous, especially in the early stages of training, by enhancing simple movements. This applies especially in the trot when lengthened strides are required. However, as training progresses and collection is required, a big, moving horse can find it difficult

Relaxed, with a job well done.

to shorten and produce a truly collected outline and will need much more time to achieve this ability.

Conformation Problems Any major faults in conformation can also produce limitations in the horse's performance. For example, the horse with a very short neck is never going to be able to lengthen it beyond its natural length. There can be many types of these problems and they can produce a number of situations that will influence and restrict the progression of training.

The ideal or perfect horse probably does not exist; there will always be some problem to overcome, however small. The same can be said about riders. No one is perfect; we can only strive continually for perfection in the hope of achieving some of the necessary qualities for the job.

When the horse is well established in his medium work, he can be introduced to the wearing of the double bridle. If the rider has no wish to compete, this is not a necessity as it is only a requirement of competition. The rider must never introduce the double bridle as a means of taking short cuts or substituting good riding and gaining submission through the use of the curb. When it is first used, the horse's work must be kept straightforward and uncomplicated until he accepts the extra control applied by its action. It can even be a good idea to take the horse for a hack on the first occasion it is worn to ensure that he has the desire to go forward. Although the horse might get used to the double bridle and work happily in it, accepting its action, it is not necessary for him to wear it every day. In fact, it must always be possible to return to the use of the snaffle and perform all work and movements with the accuracy and submission obtained with the double.

The rider must never forget that if a problem is encountered at any stage of training, little will be achieved by fighting with the horse to force his responses. Far better to re-establish the previous lesson to ensure it was well learnt and understood before trying to proceed to the next one. This will prove to be a much quicker solution in the long run and the only way that true, sound riding can progress to the next level.

Aids The use of hands, legs, seat and voice create the aids which are used to communicate messages to the horse.

Arena Dressage arenas are of two dimensions, 20m × 40m and 20m × 60m.

Balance A horse is balanced when he is upright from left to right and when his weight is carried equally on forehand and quarters.

Basic paces The basic paces are the walk, trot and canter.

Bend The curve produced laterally through the horse from head to tail.

Braced Involves the tightening and arching of the back muscles to increase the rider's aids through the back.

Collection The act of 'shortening' the horse so that he takes shorter, slightly more elevated strides.

Contact The feel maintained from the hands along the reins to the bit.

Counter canter Changing direction in the canter but not changing the leading leg.

Diagonals In the trot the horse jumps from one pair of diagonal legs to the other pair – these pairs of legs are referred to as 'the diagonals'.

Diagonal line The line from one corner of the arena across to the opposite corner.

Dressage The name given to the job of schooling the horse on the flat.

Drive An action with the rider's legs to produce energy from the horse.

Engaged The horse is said to be engaged when he places his hind legs well under his body so that they carry a good proportion of his weight.

Flexion The submissive hinging of the horse's head to the neck, both up and down and from side to side.

Forehand The front of the horse including head, neck, and shoulders.

Forward seat A more forward position adopted by a rider for jumping and fast work.

Going large The act of riding around the perimeter of the arena.

Gullet The space created between the jowl of the lower jaw, and the under neck.

Half halt The act of almost halting the horse but driving him forward again immediately as he reduces pace.

Half marker   A point half-way along the long side of a dressage arena.

Half pass   A movement performed in schooling the horse where he traverses a line by travelling both sideways and forwards.

Hollow   Relating to the outline of the horse where the head is raised and the hind legs are not engaged.

Jog   A series of short trot steps; sometimes a difficult habit to break.

Lateral aids   The aids that push or drive the horse sideways.

Lateral movements   Movements where the horse travels both sideways and forwards.

Leading leg   The leg that appears to precede the others in movement during the canter.

Leg aid   An action made with the legs to convey the rider's wishes to the horse.

Leg yield   A movement made by the horse when he is driven forwards and sideways by the rider's inside leg.

Long side   Refers to the long sides of the dressage arena.

On the bit   When the horse is accepting the contact of the bit and working into its feel.

Outline   The overall picture of the shape in which a horse is working.

Overbent   The action where the horse over-arches the neck and in so doing he brings the head back in towards the chest.

'Pace'   The action created by the horse when instead of moving diagonal legs in the trot he moves the lateral legs together.

Paces   The basic paces are the walk, trot and canter.

Renvers   A movement where the horse is placed on a diagonal line to the long side of the arena with the head pointing into the arena and bent to the direction being travelled.

Rhythm   The regularity with which the horse places his feet on the ground.

School   The action of educating the horse.

School   Referring to the riding school (arena)

Shoulder-in   A movement where the horse is asked to move his shoulders to the inside of the line being ridden.

Step   The movement involving one footfall within the stride.

Stride   The action of moving all four feet to complete a set sequence.

Submission The act of the horse obeying to the feel of the bit in his mouth.

Suspension The moment in some paces when the horse has all four feet off the ground.

Tempo The speed at which a horse travels through each complete stride.

Three-quarter line A line parallel to the long side of the arena, but three-quarters of the way across its width.

Top line The line along the top of the horse's outline from the ears to the tail.

Track The line on which a horse is ridden around the arena's edge.

Transition The act of moving from one tempo, pace or movement to another.

Travers A movement where the horse's quarters are placed to the inside of the line being ridden and he is bent to the direction in which he is moving.

Volte The smallest circle ridden on a horse which is 6m in diameter.

Yielding The action of giving with the hands on the rein to lighten the contact on the mouth.

Association of British Riding Schools,
Miss A Lawton
Old Brewery Yard
Penzance
Cornwall   TR18 2SL

British Horse Society,
British Equestrian Centre,
Stoneleigh,
Kenilworth,
Warwickshire   CV8 2LR

British Field Sports Association
General J Hopkinson
59 Kennington Road
London   SE1 7PZ

**British Show Hack, Cob and
Riding Horse Association**
Mrs R Smith
Rockwood
Packington Park
Meriden
Warwickshire   CV7 7HF

British Show Jumping Association
A R Finding
British Equestrian Centre
Stoneleigh
Kenilworth
Warwickshire   CV8 2LR

British Warmblood Society
Mrs D Wallin
Moorlands Farm
New Yatt
Witney
Oxfordshire   OX8 6TE

**Hunters Improvement and National
Light Horse Breeding Society**
G W Evans
96 High Street
Edenbridge
Kent   TN8 5AR

National Equine Welfare Committee
c/o Bronsby Home of Rest for Horses
Bransbury
Near Saxilby
Lincolnshire   LN1 2PH

National Foaling Bank
Meretown Stud
Newport
Shropshire   TF10 8BX

National Stud
Newmarket
Suffolk   CB8 0XE

Riding for the Disabled Association
Avenue R
National Agricultural Centre
Stoneleigh
Kenilworth
Warwickshire   CV8 2LY

Royal Agricultural Society of England
A D Callaghan
National Agricultural Centre
Stoneleigh
Kenilworth
Warwickshire   CV8 2LZ

Side Saddle Association
Mrs M James
Highbury House
Welford
Northamptonshire   NW6 7HT

Worshipful Company of Saddlers
The Clerk
Saddlers Hall
Gutter Lane
Cheapside
London   EC2V 6BR

Decarpentry, General, *Piaffer and Passage* (J. A. Allen, 1964)

Harris, Charles, *Fundamentals of Riding* (J. A. Allen, 1985)

Klimke, Reiner, *Basic Training of the Young Horse* (J. A. Allen, 1985)

McBane, Susan, Ed., *The Horse and the Bit* (The Crowood Press, 1988)

Museler, W., *Riding Logic* (Paul Parey Verlag, 1987)

Oliverra, Nuno, *Reflections of Equestrian Art* (J. A. Allen 1976)

Podhajsky, Alois, *The Complete Training of Horse and Rider* (George G. Harrap, 1967)

Podhajsky, Alois, *The White Stallions of Vienna* (The Sportsman's Press, 1963)

Vavra, Robert, *Such is the Real Nature of Horses* (William Collins, 1979)

Watjen, Richard L., *Dressage Riding* (J. A. Allen, 1958)